Tantalizing Tidbits for Teens 2:

More Quick Booktalks for the Busy High School Library Media Specialist

Ruth E. Cox-Clark, Ph.D.

Professional Development Resources for K-12
Library Media and Technology Specialists

Library of Congress Cataloging-in-Publication Data

Cox-Clark, Ruth E.
  Tantalizing tidbits for teens 2 : more quick booktalks for the busy high school library media specialist / Ruth E. Cox-Clark.
       p. cm.
  Includes bibliographical references and index.
     ISBN 1-58683-235-2 (pbk.)
  1. Book talks--United States. 2. High school libraries--Activity programs--United States. 3. Teenagers--Books and reading--United States. 4. Young adult literature--Bibliography. I. Title.
  Z1003.15.C693 2007
  028.5'5--dc22

2007010776

Linworth Books:
Cynthia Anderson, Book Editor
Carol Simpson, Editorial Director
Judi Repman, Associate Editor

Published by Linworth Publishing, Inc.
3650 Olentangy River Road, Suite 250
Columbus, Ohio 43214

Copyright © 2007 by Linworth Publishing, Inc.

All rights reserved. Purchasing this book entitles a librarian to reproduce activity sheets for use in the library within a school or entitles a teacher to reproduce activity sheets for single classroom use within a school. Other portions of the book (up to 15 pages) may be copied for staff development purposes within a single school. Standard citation information should appear on each page. The reproduction of any part of this book for an entire school or school system or for commercial use is strictly prohibited. No part of this book may be electronically reproduced, transmitted, or recorded without written permission from the publisher.

ISBN 1-58683-235-2

Table of Contents

About the Author v

Dedication v

Section 1. Introduction 1
    Audience 1
    Book Entry Format 2
        Bibliographic Information 2
        Web Site 2
        Subjects 3
        Genres 3
        Award 3
        Lists 3
        Levels 4
        Annotation 4
        Booktalk 4
        Excerpt 5
        Curriculum Connections 5
        Similar Titles 5
    Collaboration with Classroom Teachers 6

Section 2. Annual Recommended Reading Lists 7
    The Young Adult Library Services Association (YALSA) Lists 7
        Best Books for Young Adults 8
        Popular Paperbacks 8
        Quick Picks for Reluctant Young Adult Readers 8
        Selected Audiobooks for Young Adults 8
    The International Reading Association
        Young Adults' Choices Lists 9

Section 3. The Michael L. Printz Award 11

Section 4. Booktalking Techniques 13
    Booktalking Styles 14
        Excerpt 14
        Discussion 14
        First Person 15

Personal Style 16
　　　Before and After the Booktalk 16

Section 5. Booktalks 19

Section 6. Indices 113
　　　Authors 113
　　　Authors, Similar Titles 115
　　　Titles 123
　　　Titles, Similar 125
　　　Subjects 134
　　　Genres 137
　　　Curriculum Connections 138

Section 7. Appendix: Student Evaluation Form 139
　　　Booktalk Evaluation Form 140

About the Author

Ruth Cox-Clark, Ph.D. is an Associate Professor in the College of Education, Library Science and Instructional Technology Department at East Carolina University in Greenville, North Carolina. She teaches children's and young adult literature courses. Previously held positions include assistant professorships in library science programs at the University of Houston-Clear Lake and Sam Houston State University, a School District Library Services Directorship in Wisconsin, as well as various K-12 building level school library media specialist positions in Alaska, Texas, and the U.S. Virgin Islands. Literature committee appointments include the Young Adult Library Services Association's Best Books for Young Adults, Michael L. Printz Award, and Margaret A. Edwards Award committees as well as the Association of Library Services for Children's Newbery Award and Carnegie Award committees.

Dedication

To my wonderful, supportive husband, Steven Clark. This one is for you, Hon! Thanks for putting up with the hours I have spent reading and writing rather than with you.

Introduction

Tantalizing Tidbits for Teens 2 is a professional tool to assist busy high school library media specialists and others who work with young adults. The goal, as with the first edition, is to entice teens to slow down a bit and curl up with a good book. Sharing booktalks, such as the 75 included in this book, with busy teens who don't seem to have time to browse the fiction shelves on their own could open doors to new genres, introduce characters they may not have found on their own, or even help them discover new worlds. This resource, with an extensive list of 425 similar titles, five per title, can also be used for reader's advisory services and for collection development.

A. Audience

Because the primary audience for *Tantalizing Tidbits for Teens 2* is high school library media specialists, the novels included are appropriate for library media center collections for grades 9 through 12. Books with grade 9 as the highest suggested interest level in review sources are not included in this collection of booktalks as many school districts include ninth grade as part of the junior high school. The intent is to include booktalks that appeal to older teens, ages 15 through 18, but some of these titles will also appeal to younger teens.

The suggested interest level information has been confirmed in review sources such as *Booklist*, *Kirkus Review*, *KLIATT*, LIBRARY MEDIA CONNECTION, *Publishers*

Weekly, School Library Journal, and *Voice of Youth Advocates (VOYA).* Whenever possible, more than one review source level is listed.

The titles included are intended for older teen readers; therefore, some of the chosen books may be considered controversial. To ensure that these books are appropriate for high school library media centers, many are on the American Library Association and the International Reading Association recommended reading lists that target teens. Others have been positively reviewed, are favorites to booktalk by the author, or are newly published titles that have not yet been chosen for one of the lists. Please keep in mind that it is each school library media specialist's responsibility to determine which of these titles she feels comfortable booktalking. Always read a book before booktalking it.

B. Book Entry Format

The entries in *Tantalizing Tidbits for Teens 2* are similarly formatted, but they may vary in number of elements. For example, if a book is not a Michael L. Printz Award winner or honor book, the entry will not include an award element. Exclusion of an element means there is no information available at the time *Tantalizing Tidbits for Teens 2* is published. Also, please be aware that books go out of print in the hardback format or new paperback editions become available on a regular basis. For this reason, editions included in the bibliographic information may have gone out of print or newer editions may be available since the publication of this resource. The title entry elements are described below.

1. Bibliographic Information

Each entry includes bibliographic information for editions that are currently in print in hardback, paperback, and unabridged audiobook formats. It is common for a popular young adult title to be out of print in hardback format but to stay in print for many years in the paperback format, with numerous reprints and changes in cover art. The bibliographic information for the hardback edition is followed by the paperback and the audiobook edition, tapes followed by CDs if both audiobook formats are available. Although many audiobooks are now available in downloadable MP3 format, the audiobook additions to the citations have been limited to tape and CD formats as they can be readily purchased through most school library media vendors. Audiobooks are excellent additions to high school library media collections as they meet the needs of ESL students, learning disabled students, and those teens who prefer to listen to books. The 10-digit ISBNs and prices are included to assist in the purchasing process.

2. Web Site

Author Web sites have been included whenever possible to assist the library media specialist in locating information on authors and their books. The sites listed are specific to the author and do not include general publisher Web sites that may have information about the author or book. The author Web sites can be shared with teachers and bookmarked on the library media center computers to encourage readers to learn more about their favorite authors. Be aware that Web site URLs change frequently as does the content of Web sites. Bookmarked sites should be checked on a regular basis.

3. Subjects
A minimum of one subject is listed for each entry. These are not Library of Congress subject headings in all cases, but rather subjects requested by teachers or teen readers when they visit the library media center and request books on a specific topic or for leisure reading. For example, the psychology teacher may request a booktalking session on books that address issues covered in class such as mental illness, pregnancy, and suicide; or, a student may request a novel about sibling rivalry or a specific sport. The various subjects are accessible via the Subject Index.

4. Genres
Along with subject and curriculum requests, school library media specialists often receive requests for books in a particular genre. For example, a booktalking session for a history teacher may include historical fiction set during a specific time period. A genre, and in some cases more than one, is listed for each entry. These genres extend beyond the basic fiction genres to include listings for international and multicultural titles. This assists the library media specialist and teacher in locating titles about specific cultural groups in the United States as well as books set in countries other than the United States.

The author has not tried to balance the number of books included in *Tantalizing Tidbits for Teens 2* in terms of genre coverage. The titles were chosen for suitability in a high school library media collection and for ease of booktalking.

5. Award
If the book has received the Michael L. Printz Award or is an honor book, this is listed along with the year received. Please see Section 3: The Michael L. Printz Award for a description of this award.

6. Lists
The American Library Association (ALA) or International Reading Association (IRA) book list name and year are listed. Some titles will appear on more than one book list. A title may be on the Young Adult Library Services Association's (YALSA) Best Books for Young Adults list, the Quick Picks for Reluctant Young Adult Readers list, and also on a later year's Popular Paperbacks list. At the American Library

Association's annual conferences in 1994, 2000, and 2005, young adult literature professionals examined the previous years' Best Books for Young Adults' lists and created a Best of the Best Books list. *Tantalizing Tidbits for Teens 2* has added Selected Audiobooks for Young Adults to the YALSA lists noted here due to the strong interest in audiobooks by teen readers.

In a small number of cases the books that are on the YALSA lists also appear on the IRA's Young Adults' Choices list. This list is unique as the titles included on the annual Young Adults' Choices list have been read and voted on by teens, unlike the YALSA lists, which includes titles recommended by committees of young adult literature specialists.

Titles without a list entry may have been nominated for one of the lists, are too new to be on a list, or are favorite booktalking titles of the author. Please see Section 2: Annual Recommended Reading Lists for a description of the recommended book lists.

7. Levels

The review journal(s) and the suggested interest level ranges are included as grade levels, not ages. Some of the interest level ranges will include grades below high school. The selection criteria for the books included in *Tantalizing Tidbits for Teens 2* does not preclude including those titles suggested for readers in ninth grade or below but the suggested range, in at least one review source, must include tenth grade or above. Please note that reviewer grade level suggestions are just that, suggestions. The suggested interest level ranges among the review journals may vary considerably. The final decision for inclusion in a collection or appropriateness for a booktalk falls with the school library media specialist, after taking into account the needs and interests of the library media center users, both students and faculty.

8. Annotation

Each entry includes an annotation because booktalks are meant to entice, not to give details. Unlike the potential teen reader, the school library media specialist selecting titles to booktalk, recommend to teens, or add to the collection needs more information about the book's content than a booktalk should give. The annotation will include a basic plot summary, the age of the protagonist, and the setting whenever possible.

9. Booktalk

An attention-getting booktalk in first person or discussion style is included. Please see Section 4: Booktalking Techniques for further information on the different styles of booktalks, as well as hints for preparing and presenting booktalks.

10. Excerpt
A page range of text that may be used in an excerpt style booktalk is included for each entry. The pages listed are for the hardback edition unless otherwise noted. The suggested excerpts are included as an additional way for a high school library media specialist to highlight the books included in this resource.

11. Curriculum Connections
Suggested curriculum connections are included as general extension activities to relate the content of the book to one or more curriculum areas but are not matched to specific standards. The activities relate to one element or incident in the book or they are more general in nature, but all of the activities include a research element to encourage library media center involvement. These activities may also be modified and used as discussion starters with book clubs. The school library media specialist should be an integral part of the school faculty and the curriculum connection activities can be used to encourage collaboration between the classroom teacher and the library media specialist.

12. Similar Titles
A list of five author, genre, or subject area similar titles concludes each entry. The suggested titles may include both nonfiction and fiction. General bibliographic information is included for each title, but high school library media specialists should check for suitability for their particular library media center.

The similar titles do not include books with entries in *Tantalizing Tidbits for Teens 2*, nor are any of the similar titles listed in more than one entry. The intent of including a list of five similar titles for each entry is to assist the school library media specialist in quickly pulling together a group of books to supplement the titles being booktalked. For example, a booktalk on five of the books included in *Tantalizing Tidbits for Teens 2* results in a list of 25 similar books that can be offered to the students. These similar titles may also be used for collection development and reader's advisory services for teens as there are an additional 425 similar titles included.

Some of the similar titles are newly published but many are well-known older titles that will likely be in the collection. Although the bibliographic information for a title included in this professional resource may list only a paperback edition currently in print, the library media center may have an older hardback edition on the shelves.

C. Collaboration with Classroom Teachers

The curriculum connection and subject information are included for each book to assist the school library media specialist in putting together booktalking sessions of various types. The library media specialist may browse through *Tantalizing Tidbits for Teens 2* for booktalks to introduce students to a wide variety of books. The specific entry information and the indices may also be used to select titles for curriculum-related booktalking sessions. Browsing through and reading booktalks that look interesting is certainly an excellent way to become familiar with this booktalking tool, but the author, title, subject, genre, and curriculum connections indices greatly enhance its usability.

Tantalizing Tidbits for Teens 2 should be shared with teachers. The entries include research-based activities as suggested ways to extend the experience with a book beyond reading and discussing it in class. These extension activities may spark students' interest in learning more about the time period, setting, or subjects introduced in the novel. Students use the school library media center to locate information they need for assignments, but that is not all that goes on in a school library media center. Integrating literature into the curriculum and helping create lifelong readers and researchers who extend their knowledge beyond the novel itself are part of what proactive school library media specialists do on a daily basis. The curriculum connection activities include a research element to encourage collaboration by the classroom teacher and the library media specialist, but they are also meant to help students make the connection between enjoyable reading experiences and potential research activities.

Annual Recommended Reading Lists

Thousands of books for young people are published each year in the United States, with the Wikipedia entry on Young Adult Literature <http://en.wikipedia.org/wiki/Young_adult_literature#Publishing_market> suggesting approximately 400 Young Adult (YA) titles were published annually as of 2004. Professional journals such as *Booklist, Kirkus Review, KLIATT, Library Media Connection, Publishers Weekly, School Library Journal,* and *Voice of Youth Advocates (VOYA)* include reviews of books appropriate for young adult readers. Reviews were read to determine high school interest levels. As well as highly reviewed, many of the titles included in *Tantalizing Tidbits for Teens 2* are recommendations of YA literature professionals or are the choices of teen readers, appearing on the YALSA's Best Books for Young Adults, Popular Paperbacks, Quick Picks for Reluctant Young Adult Readers, and Selected Audiobooks lists as well as the International Reading Association's Young Adults' Choices lists. Teen-created lists found on Barnes and Noble <www.barnesandnoble.com> and Amazon <www.amazon.com> Web sites were also perused to help select high-interest titles.

A. The Young Adult Library Services Association (YALSA) Lists

The titles on the Best Books for Young Adults, the Popular Paperbacks, the Quick Picks for Reluctant Young Adult Readers, and the Selected Audiobooks lists are chosen by committees of professionals in the area of young adult literature who are also members of the Young Adult Library Services Association (YALSA), a division of the American Library Association (ALA). Along with novels, the lists also include informational books, biographies, poetry collections, and short story collections. Information about the Young Adult Library Services Association and its services is available at <www.ala.org/yalsa>.

1. Best Books for Young Adults

The Best Books for Young Adults annual list presents books marketed for adults and young adults that were published within the previous 16 months and are recommended reading for teens. The lists are available at <www.ala.org/ala/yalsa/booklistsawards/bestbooksya/bestbooksyoung.htm>.

2. Popular Paperbacks

The Popular Paperbacks committee annually prepares one to five annotated list(s) of at least 10, but no more than 25, recommended titles selected from popular genres, topics, or themes. The intent of the list is to present teens with a selection of popular titles representing a broad variety of themes and subjects that are readily accessible in paperback format. There is no limit on the copyright date of the titles included as long as they are in print in paperback format. The lists are available at <www.ala.org/ala/yalsa/booklistsawards/popularpaperback/popularpaperbacks.htm>.

3. Quick Picks for Reluctant Young Adult Readers

The Quick Picks for Reluctant Young Adult Readers committee prepares an annual annotated list of recommended books published in the last 18 months that are appropriate for reluctant teen readers. These titles are intended for recreational reading, not for remedial or curricular use. The titles should have self-selection appeal for teens. The subject matter, cover art, readability, format, and style are considered when nominating and voting on titles. The lists are available at <www.ala.org/ala/yalsa/booklistsawards/quickpicks/quickpicksreluctant.htm>.

4. Selected Audiobooks for Young Adults

The members of the Selected Audiobooks for Young Adults committee prepares an annual annotated list of recommended audiobooks released in the past two years with content that will appeal to young adult listeners. Curricular suitability may be considered but is not a requirement for inclusion. The lists are available at <www.ala.org/ala/yalsa/booklistsawards/selectedaudio/selectedaudiobooks.htm>.

B. The International Reading Association Young Adults' Choices List

Teen readers from around the United States choose the 30 books on the annual Young Adults' Choices list. Each year the International Reading Association selects team leaders from five different regions of the United States. The team leaders then choose several secondary schools within their areas to receive books marketed for young adults. Publishers send books that have received two positive reviews in recognized review journals to the team leaders who coordinate the placement of these books in the schools chosen for inclusion in the project. The teens self select titles and vote on their favorites. The 30 books, fiction or nonfiction, with the most votes become the list, which is then annotated by the members of the Literature for Young Adults Committee. The lists are available at <www.reading.org/resources/tools/choices_young_adults.html>.

The Michael L. Printz Award

The Michael L. Printz Award recognizes literary excellence in young adult literature. The selection committee annually names one award book and as many as four honor books. The books must be published between January 1 and December 31 of the prior year and be designated as a young adult book by the publisher or published for the age range of 12 through 18. The books may be fiction, nonfiction, poetry, or an anthology and may have been previously published in another country. More information about this award can be found at www.ala.org/ala/yalsa/booklistsawards/printzaward/Printz,_Michael_L__Award.htm>.

SECTION 4

Booktalking Techniques

Mike Printz, the high school library media specialist for whom the Michael L. Printz Award is named, said in a September 1993 interview included in *School Library Journal's Best* (Neal-Schuman, 1997) that booktalking to a group of high school students is one of the greatest motivational tools a high school library media specialist has. He stated that, "Of all the things I've ever done, that would have to be the greatest rush in the world. To be able to talk about books and turn somebody on; to have them come up and almost pull the book out of your hand or knock you over to pick up the book because they want to read."

This author, after many years of booktalking with teens, has to agree with Printz that booktalking is a wonderful motivational tool to entice high school students to read, but only if the booktalker keeps their attention. A lengthy booktalk that "tells it all" will not have teens rushing up to get the books as they did when Printz booktalked to them. He was a pro. He knew how to find an element or event in a book that would relate to teens' lives. Booktalking is as easy as tying your shoes for some school library media specialists or as difficult as doing calculus in your head for others. The booktalks included in *Tantalizing Tidbits for Teens 2* are short enough to be memorized by the novice booktalker or may be used as style hints for the pro. Each of the entries also includes a suggested section of text to use in an excerpt booktalk to help the novice booktalker become more comfortable with the booktalking process.

Booktalking is a lot like acting, but in this case the booktalker is also the writer, the producer, and the director. There is no off-scene director shouting, "Cut!" if the booktalker deviates from the script. Some booktalkers work from outlines or notes and others have actual "scripts" that they memorize. There is no right or wrong way to prepare for a booktalk, but preparation is a must. A booktalker should not present an unread book. The teen who enjoyed a booktalked title may want to discuss the book and request more like it. A booktalker who has read the book and similar titles to recommend for further reading can discuss the book in as much detail as the reader desires and can also suggest other books that might be of interest. The impact of a booktalk goes far beyond the short duration in which it is presented.

A. Booktalking Styles

Booktalks are as unique as the person presenting them, but basically there are three styles of booktalks most often given—the excerpt, the discussion, and the first person.

1. Excerpt

The excerpt is the easiest. Find a juicy tidbit of text and read it aloud to the students, leaving them with a cliffhanger. The excerpt should have the audience wanting more. Leave them wanting to know what happens next. When reading a book, a booktalker should keep page flags available to mark passages for future booktalks. Remember to also write the page(s) down elsewhere, since the book being shared will more than likely be checked out at the conclusion of the booktalk. The excerpt style of booktalk is not present in *Tantalizing Tidbits for Teens 2* but each entry includes a suggested section of text to use in an excerpt style booktalk.

Choose excerpts wisely. A booktalker's head is down while reading aloud and it is easy to lose the connection with your audience. Eye contact is an essential part of booktalking as it helps a booktalker read the audience's response. Their facial expressions give immediate feedback on whether or not to shorten or to expand upon a particular booktalk, perhaps even asking for audience interaction to encourage involvement.

2. Discussion

The discussion booktalk takes a bit more work on the booktalker's part. The booktalker shares tidbits of the plot, setting, character, or an intriguing incident from the book to get teens' attention. The booktalker is basically talking about the book and sometimes even asks the audience a short question or two to get them involved. However, requesting too much discussion can cause the group to lose focus, or in the case of a group unknown to the booktalker, make the group uncomfortable about being asked to interact. Reading the audience for their response to a request for interaction is essential. In most cases questions that require a yes or no response are enough to get the audience's attention and involvement.

For example, the booktalk included for Martha Books' *True Confessions of a Heartless Girl* begins with the question, "Have any of you ever felt like no matter what you did it turned out wrong?" Since most of us have felt this way at some point in our lives, the audience will respond with a nod of their head or perhaps even a resounding, "Yes!" from the more interactive participants. The booktalker has hooked the audience's attention immediately as they already feel a kinship to the character and they don't know a thing about her yet.

3. First Person

The first person booktalk takes some acting skill on the booktalker's part. While presenting this style of booktalk, the booktalker becomes one of the characters in the book and talks to the audience as the character.

First person novels such as Joyce Carol Oates' *Freaky Green Eyes* are the easiest to create a first person booktalk for because the main character's voice is so strong, but a first person booktalk is different from reading an excerpt from a book written in first person. The booktalker actually writes the script and acts as the character in the book. A first person booktalk for *Freaky Green Eyes* may begin with an introduction: "I'm Francesca Pierson, but most people call me Franky. What they don't know is that I renamed myself on my 14th birthday, or I should say the guy who I had to fight off at a party I wasn't even supposed to be at, renamed me. When I fought back he said I had Freaky Green Eyes. I don't know where that strong side of me came from, but I liked it. I fought him off and I felt powerful—I was Freaky Green Eyes!"

Can a booktalker present a first person booktalk in which the character is the opposite sex? Yes, it is acceptable, and in many cases downright fun. The audience certainly sits up and pays attention while they are trying to figure out what the booktalker is doing. As a "slightly older than teenage" female, this author loves to present first person booktalks with teenage male protagonists for books such as David Klass' *Firestorm* that starts out:

"Let me tell you about myself. My name is Jack Danielson. Pretty normal name, right? I thought I was a typical senior guy in high school with the typical hobbies—chicks, flicks, and fast cars. In that order. Oh yeah—and sports. Left that out, but I am a natural at sports. I am the starting running back on the football team. Of course I am. I'm 6'2"..."

At this point half of the guys in the audience are cracking up as I am 5'3" and look quite comical acting like a cocky football player as I present this booktalk, but I have done what a good booktalker sets out to do—get their attention. Presenting a first person booktalk may seem daunting to the novice booktalker but many discover that it is their favorite style, as well as the audience's favorite, as it is not the normal presentation style used to introduce books to teens. Teens have been read to for most of their school career and having a teacher or library media specialist discuss a book is not unusual, but listening to a first person booktalk is an experience many of them have not had before.

4. Personal Style

Each booktalker finds her own unique personal style with practice, but it is wise to vary the types of booktalks given in a session covering several books. If excerpts are read from every book, the audience will get bored. It is a good idea to move around, at least in the front of the room, if not among the audience.

It is also essential to create interesting transitions between books, rather than saying "And my next book is…" each time. Use transitions to connect the books, highlighting similarities in the characters or situations they are experiencing. Smoothly move from one book to another so the audience views the session as a whole rather than a group of disjointed talks on several books. The transitions will also keep you from concluding booktalks with "you'll have to read the book to find out" type of statement as a booktalk is meant to do just that, entice the listener to read the book.

B. Before and After the Booktalking Session

Novice booktalkers may want to videotape themselves presenting sample booktalks to critique their booktalking style as well as detect distracting mannerisms and body movements. Little things you are not even aware of will show up on the video, such as the repeated use of "um," "like," and other filler words or the self-conscious fingering of a ring or necklace.

Some booktalkers put their notes on the back of the books but there is potential for problems with this technique. Novice booktalkers may inadvertently hold the book up in front of their face when referring to the notes, which is very distracting to the audience as they want to see the booktalker's enthusiasm for the book that is being addressed. The notes will also need to be removed from the books so the teens can check them out. Instead, print out the booktalks or notes in a large font and place them where they can be referred to without picking them up. Most booktalkers find once they start talking about the books, the notes are there just for back up.

The booktalker should also be attentive to how and where the book is being held so that the audience can see the cover. Smooth verbal transitions should be made between books as one is set down and another picked up. Prior to beginning the session, make sure the books are in order so the flow is not broken by searching for the next title. Avoid making statements such as "I really liked this book" or "I wasn't crazy about this book, but someone your age might be." Focus on the book itself, not your opinion of it. The audience assumes the booktalker read and liked the book.

Although multiple copies may be available in the library, including some that are tattered and torn, a visually attractive copy should be used for the booktalk. The paperback edition cover art often has more teen appeal than the hardback. Holding up a hardback edition with the dust jacket missing will not garner interest. There is no visual appeal to a gray or navy book cover. Teens, like readers of any age, often select books because they find the cover art attractive. Even if the copy they check out is missing the cover, they have seen what the cover looks like during the booktalk.

Clearly state the author and title of the book to help the audience remember the book for later reference. Most booktalkers state the author and title both before and after the booktalk. Handing out a list of the books, with catchy one-line annotations for each title, prior to the booktalking session also helps. Consider putting the title of the book first, rather than the author's name, since most listeners can more quickly find the book on the list by title. Also, teens are more likely to remember the title of a book than the author. Include similar titles on the list, as more than likely there won't be enough copies of the booktalked titles to meet reader demand. Each entry in *Tantalizing Tidbits for Teens 2* includes a list of five similar titles to assist in this process.

A book cart or a display of the booktalked books and similar titles alleviates the frustration that may occur when students get excited about a book but cannot check it out due to a waiting list. Add audiobook copies of the popular booktalked titles to the collection. Also consider sharing the book list with the public library and the local bookstore so they will be prepared for those readers with public library cards or those who want to buy the books.

The specific audience and the booktalking environment will determine the length of the session. A short informal booktalk on a single book may take place in the library media center or even in the school hallway. It may also be a lengthy pre-arranged booktalking session for a particular group of students. Thirty minutes is a suitable length of time to booktalk to a group of students. Approximately 10-15 titles can be shared in a 30-minute session, but more books than can be booktalked during the session should be available. A booktalker may talk faster than planned or the audience's response may indicate that some of the planned booktalks are not good choices. Also, allow time for the students to ask questions and to browse through the books.

Booktalks are logistically easier for the school library media specialist to do in the library media center, but many teachers do not have the time to take their students to the library media center. In a large high school it may take a good portion of the class period to walk to the library media center and get the students seated. On the other hand, the library media specialist can be waiting in the classroom, prepared to start booktalking as soon as the students are seated. The goal is to "advertise" as many of the books in the library media center as possible. Also, visiting the classrooms gives the library media specialist additional visibility in the school.

At the conclusion of the booktalking session, a booktalker should ask the teacher and students for input. If a particular booktalk did not go over well with the audience, it may not have been the book but rather the booktalk style. See the sample Student Evaluation Form in the Appendix.

A booktalker should make notes about the session as soon as possible after the session and keep the original of the book list for later use. Note the date and to whom the booktalk was presented to keep from repeating booktalks with the same group of students. Keeping electronic notes for each session, along with an electronic copy of the handout so it can be adapted for later use, tends to be the most effective way to keep up with the tracking process.

Individual booktalks should also be saved electronically for later use. Some booktalkers print them out and sort them by topic in three-ring binders with a booktalk per page. Others create a database with the author, title, booktalk, the class presented to, and a column for notes about the session. Whatever the filing and storage system used, a wealth of booktalks can be compiled and adapted.

Booktalking should be an integral element of the high school library media program, not only to present curriculum-related titles by teacher request, but also to present titles for teens' leisure reading. In addition to group booktalks, offer to present short booktalks during the morning announcements and design a special display for these books. If there is a TV studio in the school, offer to present booktalks on the air and assist students in writing and broadcasting their own booktalks. Offer to work with teachers to create and present booktalks to share with their students for the age-appropriate books they are personally reading, as well as encourage them to offer booktalking to students as an alternative to a book report.

Using booktalking to highlight the leisure reading materials in the library media center is an essential element in high schools that is often overlooked because of the extensive use of the high school library media center for research projects and curriculum-related assignments. Presenting booktalking sessions both in the library media center and in the classroom encourages students to self select leisure reading materials as well as to develop their love of books, which helps result in lifelong readers. Reading promotion goes hand in hand with teaching information literacy skills at all levels of education, including high school.

Booktalks

Abbreviations used in this section:

B of BBYA	Best of the Best Books for Young Adults
BBYA	Best Books for Young Adults
BL	*Booklist*
K	*Kirkus Review*
KL	*KLIATT*
LMC	*Library Media Connection*
PP	Popular Paperbacks for Young Adults
PW	*Publishers Weekly*
QP	Quick Picks for Reluctant Young Adult Readers
SA	Selected Audiobooks for Young Adults
SLJ	*School Library Journal*
V	*Voice of Youth Advocates*
YAC	Young Adults' Choices

The following entries are numbered and listed in alphabetical order by the author's last name. The indexes refer to entry numbers rather than page numbers.

1

Adlington, L.J., *The Diary of Pelly D.*
Greenwillow, 2005, 288pp. $17.89. ISBN: 0060766166.

Subjects: Genetics, Journals, Moving, Prejudices, Swimming, Testing, War, Writing
Genres: Science Fiction
Lists: 2006 BBYA
Levels: BL 8-12, KL 7-12, PW 8 up, SLJ 7-10

Annotation: In a futuristic colony on another planet, 14-year-old Toni V finds 15-year-old Pelly D's diary and learns how this once popular girl responded to the decline of her family's social status during holocaust-like changes based on genetics. Chapters alternate between the two characters' perspectives.

Booktalk: Have any of you seen an old Kevin Costner movie called *Waterworld?* In this movie Costner's character is a genetic mutant who has gills on the side of his neck that he can breathe through when he is under water. Pelly D, who lives in a colony on another planet, also has gills on her neck and loves to hang out with her friends at the swimming pool. All of the genetically altered humans who inhabit this colony have gills. Everyone evolves from three gene pools—with the Atsumisi at the top and the Galrezi at the bottom, but no one really cared about this hierarchy until the government began requiring that everyone submit to genetic testing and their gene pool emblem be boldly tattooed onto the top of their hand. Pelly D holds her breath, hoping for the red tattoo, the blood colored emblem that means she can keep her "most popular girl in school" status. No such luck. Her emblem is Galrezi green. Pelly D's world is about to change dramatically and not for the better. The government decides families, like Pelly D's, who do not bear the coveted red Atsumisi emblem must move out of their large apartments and into small communal living quarters. Pelly D's fall from grace is chronicled in her journal, which she buries in a paint can in the hope that future generations will know what those in power did to people who didn't wear the right emblem on their hand.

Excerpt: Page 71 through page 74.

Curriculum Connections: Geography, History
Schedule time in the library media center for students to research worldwide incidents of genocide. Based on their research, have students create a timeline and map of areas in the world where genocide has occurred, discussing the similarity to what happened to Pelly D's family.

Similar Titles:
Card, Orson Scott, *Ender's Shadow.* Tor, 1999, 379pp. $24.95. ISBN: 031286860X. Tor, 2000, 480pp. $7.99. ISBN: 0812575717. Audio Renaissance, 2005. $49.95. CD. ISBN: 159397664X.

Engdahl, Sylvia, ***Enchantress from the Stars.*** Walker, 2001, 288pp. $18.95. ISBN: 0802787649. Penguin, 2003, 288pp. $6.99. ISBN: 0142500372.

Engdahl, Sylvia, ***The Far Side of Evil.*** Penguin, 2005, 324pp. $6.99. ISBN: 0142402931.

Layne, Steven L., ***This Side of Paradise.*** Pelican, 2003, 224pp. $15.99. ISBN: 1589800966. Pelican, 2005, 224pp. $8.95. ISBN: 1589802543.

Nolan, Han, ***If I Should Die Before I Wake.*** Harcourt, 2003, 312pp. $6.95. ISBN: 0152046798.

Aidinoff, Elsie V., *The Garden.*

HarperCollins, 2004, 416pp. $17.89. ISBN: 0060556064. HarperTempest, 2005, 416pp. $6.99. ISBN: 0060556072.

Subjects: Animals, Journeys, Rape, Religion, Self-Esteem, Theft
Genres: Fantasy, Historical, Religious
Lists: 2005 BBYA
Levels: PW 9 up, SLJ 11 up, V 7-12

Annotation: God was lonely in the Garden of Eden and created Adam and Eve so He could be entertained and listened to, which Adam did to the best of his ability. God didn't expect Eve to be such an inquisitive young woman, whose curiosity was further piqued by the Serpent, who became her mentor.

Booktalk: God didn't like being questioned. He just assumed that since He was God that Adam and Eve would do exactly what He said. He never imagined that Eve would go against His wishes. But she did, with a bit of help. The Serpent, Eve's mentor, patiently answered all of her questions and, without God's knowledge, took Eve on trips outside the Garden. Eve collected sand from the beach, the mountains, and the desert and molded a beautiful pot but it melted in the rain. On that very spot a tree grew, a tree that God had not given permission to grow in His Garden. He was furious and tried to destroy it. When that didn't work He commanded Adam and Eve not to eat the apples from the Tree of the Knowledge of Good and Evil. The Serpent did not tell them to eat or not eat the apple, but told them of the consequences of doing so. It was their choice to make. Those apples looked awfully tempting, especially the one way up on top that neither of them could reach. Who could reach it?

Excerpt: First full paragraph on page 2 through the fourth paragraph on page 4.

Curriculum Connections: English, History
Schedule time in the library media center for students to locate other novels, short stories, and picture books that share the story of Adam and Eve and the Garden of Eden and compare them to *The Garden* in relation to how the characters' personalities vary.

Similar Titles:
Chevalier, Tracy, ***The Girl with a Pearl Earring.*** Penguin, 2000, 240pp. $21.95. ISBN: 052594527X. Penguin, 2003, 233pp. $14. ISBN: 0452284937. Recorded Books, 2001, $25.95. ISBN: 0788760440. Recorded Books, 2004, $24.95. CD. ISBN: 141931176X.
Diamant, Anita, ***The Red Tent.*** St. Martin's Press, 1997, 336pp. $24.95. ISBN: 0312169787. St. Martin's Press, 2005, 321pp. $16.95. ISBN: 0312353766. St. Martin's Press, 1998, 321pp. $14.95. ISBN: 0312195516. Audio Renaissance, 2000, $39.95. ISBN: 1559276452. Audio Renaissance, 2002, $49.95. CD. ISBN: 1559277092.
Hautman, Pete, ***Godless.*** Simon & Schuster, 2004, 208pp. $15.95. ISBN: 0689862784. Simon & Schuster, 2005, 198pp. $7.99. ISBN: 1416908161.
Moore, Christopher, ***Lamb: The Gospel According to Biff, Christ's Childhood Pal.*** HarperCollins, 2003, 464pp. $13.95. ISBN: 0380813815.
Willard, Nancy, ***The Tale of Paradise Lost: Based on the Poem by John Milton.*** Simon & Schuster, 2004, 150pp. $17.95. ISBN: 0689850972.

3 Bell, Hilari, *Fall of a Kingdom.*

Farsala Trilogy. Simon & Schuster, 2004, 343pp. $16.95. ISBN: 1416905456. Simon & Schuster, 2005, 448pp. $5.99. ISBN: 0689854145.

Web Site: <www.sfwa.org/members/bell>
Subjects: Brothers and Sisters, Death, Fathers and Daughters, Journeys, Magic, Royalty, Teachers, War
Genres: Adventure, Fantasy, Supernatural
Levels: BL 6-10, PW 7 up, SLJ 6-10, V 7-12

Annotation: Fifteen-year-old Lady Soraya, when sent into hiding by her father so that she will not be assassinated, is befriended by a Suud tribe and discovers she has djinn magic. Jiaan, her half brother, angered by their father's death in battle, tracks down the peddler who betrayed them. Originally entitled *Flame*.

Booktalk: Soraya is incredibly angry when she discovers her beloved father's plan to hide her away with a peasant family. The daughter of the High Commander of Farsala will not live in some pigsty. Her half-brother Jiaan ducks as a bronze cup flies past his head while he tries to assure Soraya that their father is not trying to cast her out. Instead, he has a plan to save her from being sacrificed. But Soraya is in a rage and will not listen. Another cup flies by Jiaan's head as she screams at him about being sent to some "dung-sucking outland." Suddenly Jiaan finds himself diving to catch a priceless glass bowl his spoiled sister threw at him. Jiaan shouts, "OW!" as, on his way down, another priceless plate hits him full in the chest. Soraya is too wrapped up in her anger to realize she should quiet down before she attracts the attention of the one person she is afraid of. Too late. As Soraya is about to throw a wooden horse at Jiaan the door opens and Lady Suduba walks in. Jiaan knows what will happen and abruptly leaves the room as Lady Suduba grabs Soraya's ear and viciously twists it. Jiaan is relieved Lady Saduba is not his mother. Even Jiaan knows that Lady Saduba's face will not soften for Soraya. It is evident to everyone, especially to Soraya, that Lady Saduba loves only her young son, the heir. Jiaan, the bastard son of their father, sneaks away feeling no envy for his half-sister's riches filled life with this cold and calculating woman. He'd rather live in the dung-sucking outland than with Lady Saduba!

Excerpt: First full paragraph on page 220 through page 221.

Curriculum Connections: Biology, Health, Science
The Suud people have no pigment in their skin to protect them from the sun. Schedule time in the library media center for students to research what causes albinoism as well as the effect this condition has on a person's life.

Similar Titles:
Bell, Hilari, *Forging the Sword.* Farsala Trilogy. Simon & Schuster, 2006, 512pp. $17.99. ISBN: 0689854161.
Bell, Hilari, *Rise of a Hero.* Farsala Trilogy. Simon & Schuster, 2005, 448pp. $5.99. ISBN: 0689854145
Dokey, Cameron, *The Storyteller's Daughter.* Simon & Schuster, 2002, 240pp. $5.99. ISBN: 0743422201.
Napoli, Donna Jo, *Beast.* Simon & Schuster, 2000, 272pp. $17. ISBN: 0689835892. Simon & Schuster, 2004, 272pp. $5.99. ISBN: 0689870051.
Tarnowska, Wafa, *The Seven Wise Princesses: A Medieval Persian Epic.* Barefoot Books, 2000, 96pp. $19.99. ISBN: 1841480223.

Bennett, Holly, *The Bonemender.*
Orca, 2005, 203pp. $7.95. ISBN: 155143362.
Subjects: Elves, Journeys, Magic, Medicine, Occupations, Relationships, Royalty, War
Genres: Fantasy, Romance
Levels: BL 6-9, KL 6-12, SLJ 7 up

Annotation: Gabrielle, a healer and the daughter of the royal family, falls in love with an Elvish stranger who appears at their door to warn her parents of impending war. She follows the Elf Feolan into the battlefield, healing soldiers as she searches for him.

Booktalk: How many of you have read or seen any of *The Lord of the Rings* books or movies? I love high fantasy, especially if there are Elvish characters in it, as there are in this book. The author and her children are big fans of Tolkien so this may remind you a bit of Tolkien's wonderful tales. Gabrielle is a healer, often also called a bonemender. Hence, the title of this book. She is also the daughter of the King and Queen of Verdeau. Her skill in healing with her hands and mind is far beyond that of other human bonemenders in the kingdom. Gabrielle does not know why she has such an advanced level of healing ability, nor has she ever questioned it. It is just part of who she is. Thoughts of how different she is from her parents had not entered her mind before the Elvish scouts, Danais and Feolan, appeared at the castle doors. Danais is much in need of Gabrielle's healing power due to a severe leg wound, but they have come to warn the King and Queen of impending war. Gabrielle spends most of her time with the Elves as she works on Danais's leg wound and she falls in love with Feolan. It is because of her love for and comfort level with an Elf that she begins to question if she, a human, and Feolan, an Elf, can have a future together. But thoughts of their future abruptly come to an end when the enemy army arrives. The soldiers of Verdeau and the Elves join forces against a vicious foe. It is a bloody war, with many deaths on both sides. Gabrielle, ignoring her family's fear for her safety, journeys to the battlefield to heal soldiers as she searches for Feolan, who she fears may have been wounded or killed.

Excerpt: Page 36 through page 38.

Curriculum Connections: Art, English

Novels with author-created kingdoms are often called high fantasy. Schedule time in the library media center for students to self select a high fantasy novel that does not have a map included and create a map of the fantasy realm/kingdom with sites and routes marked to indicate journeys taken by characters in the book.

Similar Titles:

Bennett, Holly, **The Bonemender's Oath.** Orca, 2006, 176pp. $7.95. ISBN: 1551434431.
Hanley, Victoria, **The Seer and the Sword.** Holiday House, 2000, 341pp. $17.95. ISBN: 0823415325. Random House, 2003, 352pp. $6.50. ISBN: 0440229774.
Jordan, Sherryl, **Secret Sacrament.** HarperCollins, 2001, 352pp. $17.89. ISBN: 0060289058.
Smith, Sherwood, **Crown Duel.** Penguin, 2002, 480pp. $7.99. ISBN: 0142301515.
Tolkien, J.R.R., **The Silmarillion.** Houghton Mifflin, 2004, 416pp. $35. ISBN: 0618391118. Houghton Mifflin, 2001, 384pp. $14. ISBN: 0618126988. Random House, 1985, 480pp. $7.99. ISBN: 0345325818. Random House Audio, 1998, $59.95. ISBN: 0553525409. Random House Audio, 1998, $64.95. CD. ISBN: 0553456067.

Bennett, James, *Faith Wish.*
Holiday House, 2003, 247pp. $16.95. ISBN: 0823417786.

Web Site: <www.jameswbennett.com>
Subjects: Attention Deficit Hyperactivity Disorder, Cults, Family Problems, Learning Disabilities, Pregnancy, Religion, Runaways, Self-Esteem, Sexual Relationships, Sisters, Suicide, Testing
Genres: Realistic, Religious
Levels: PW 6 up, SLJ 7 up, V 7-12

Annotation: Frustrated by her Attention Deficit Disorder and an inability to concentrate in school as well as her parents' pressure to excel, 17-year-old Anne-Marie turns to religion and is seduced by a young charismatic traveling preacher.

Booktalk: No matter how hard I try I can't be as good as her. Not at anything. I really do try. I just can't seem to keep my attention on anything until it's finished. It isn't like I didn't want to finish the biology paper. I did the research, but I just didn't get around to writing it. The looking up stuff part was fun, but sitting down and writing the paper just never happened. I kept getting distracted. Then my parents went ballistic because the counselor told them she thought I might have a learning disability called Attention Deficit Disorder. They were not happy that there might be a problem with my going to college. They were not happy to learn I was not going to be another perfect daughter, like my older sister. I already knew that. Deep down inside they knew it too. They just didn't want to admit that they created a child who is less than perfect. The only place I feel special is when I am with him. I hadn't really thought much about religion before I went to the revival with a friend. I certainly didn't think I would fall in love with a preacher, but I did. He has these beautiful eyes and this soft voice and when he touches me it feels wonderful. It can't be wrong, can it? He said it wasn't wrong. He said it was beautiful. Now I just need to find him. He is a traveling preacher and I have to find him. It's real important that I find him soon.

Excerpt: First full paragraph on page 40 to break on page 44.

Curriculum Connections: Biology, Health, Science
Schedule time in the library media center for students to research Attention Deficit Disorder and other medical conditions or learning disabilities such as dyslexia to compare how the brain responds to the different disorders as it processes information.

Similar Titles:
Bardi, Abby, *The Book of Fred.* Pocket, 2001, 304pp. $24. ISBN: 0743411935. Pocket, 2002, 320pp. $13. ISBN: 0743411943.
Crew, Linda, *The Brides of Eden: A True Story Imagined.* HarperCollins, 2001, 240pp. $15.89. ISBN: 0060287500.

Haddix, Margaret Peterson, **Leaving Fishers.** Simon & Schuster, 2002, 272pp. $5.99. ISBN: 068986793X.

Lewis, Richard, **The Flame Tree.** Simon & Schuster, 2004, 288pp. $16.95. ISBN: 0689863330.

Peck, Richard, **The Last Safe Place on Earth.** Random House, 2005, 176pp. $5.99. ISBN: 0440220076.

6

Black, Holly, *Tithe: A Modern Faerie Tale.*

Simon & Schuster, 2002, 320pp. $16.95. ISBN: 0689849249. Simon Pulse, 2004, 331pp. $6.99. ISBN: 0689867042.

Web Site: <www.blackholly.com>
Subjects: Cities, Elves, Fairies, Magic, Mothers and Daughters, Moving, Music, War
Genres: Fantasy
Lists: 2003 BBYA, 2005 PP
Levels: BL 8-12, PW 6 up, SLJ 9 up

Annotation: Sixteen-year-old, half-Japanese Kaye and her rock musician mother return to New Jersey where Kaye discovers that her lifelong feelings of being different and seeing faerie creatures is not her imagination. She is a faerie creature and a key element in the battle between two faerie kingdoms.

Booktalk: Although this book is set in modern day New Jersey, I could not help but visualize the blonde Elf in *The Lord of the Rings* movies when I read about handsome Roiben, the Elf knight who entered Kaye's life. Kaye found Roiben sprawled in the mud with a sword clenched in his hand. It was more than the sword that made the Elf look so out of place. It was also his pewter colored shoulder length hair and his leather armor, sculpted to look like feathers. Kaye drew in her breath when she saw a branch sticking out of his chest, the tip dark with blood. When he spoke, he asked if she had done this to him. How could she have? She had never seen him before, but she was only a little bit afraid of him. Certainly not enough to harm him. Unlike a normal human, Kaye was not at all surprised to see the pointed tips of his ears through his wet hair. She immediately knew that he was of the Faerie World. Faerie creatures were not new or foreign to Kaye. As a child she had Gristle and a group of other faerie friends who she thought were imaginary. Kaye suddenly realized her childhood pals were very real, just as real as the wounded Elf in front of her. Kaye helped Roiben pull the arrow from his chest and with this act of kindness found herself embroiled in a war between the two Courts of the Faerie World. Will Kaye hold her own in the faerie realm that she once thought of as only make believe, but is now a world in which she very much belongs?

Excerpt: Paragraph beginning on the bottom of page 13 to the first line in the last paragraph on page 16.

Curriculum Connections: Art, History
The armor that Roiben and the other fairies wear is made of hardened leather. Schedule time in the library media center for students to research the various materials that have been used to make armor. Students may also create illustrations of what they think early armor looked like, with designs such as the feather pattern on Roiben's.

Similar Titles:
Bull, Emma, ***War for the Oaks.*** Tor, 2004, 336pp. $6.99. ISBN: 0765349159.
de Lint, Charles, ***The Blue Girl.*** Viking, 2004, 384pp. $17.99. ISBN: 0670059242. Penguin, 2006, 384pp. $7.99. ISBN: 0142405450.
Lynn, Tracy, ***Snow.*** Simon & Schuster, 2003, 259pp. $5.99. ISBN: 0689855567.
Shetterly, Will, ***Nevernever.*** Harcourt, 2004, 226pp. $6.95. ISBN: 0152052100.
Zusak, Markus, ***I Am the Messenger.*** Knopf, 2005, 368pp. $16.95. ISBN: 0375830995. Knopf, 2006, 368pp. $8.95. ISBN: 0375836675. Listening Library, 2006, $39. CD. ISBN: 0739337297.

Black, Holly, *Valiant: A Modern Tale of Faerie.*
Simon & Schuster, 2005, 320pp. $16.95. ISBN: 0689868227. Simon & Schuster, 2006, 336pp. $7.99. ISBN: 0689868235. Random House Audio, 2006. $39. CD. ISBN: 0739331213.

Web Site: <www.blackholly.com>
Subjects: Cities, Drug Abuse, Fairies, Friendship, Journeys, Magic, Mothers and Daughters, Runaways, Trolls
Genres: Fantasy
Lists: 2006 BBYA, 2006 QP
Levels: BL 8-11, PW 9 up, SLJ 9 up, V 10-12

Annotation: After seeing her mother with her boyfriend, 17-year-old Valerie runs away to Manhattan, lives in a subway tunnel with other teens, gets high on Nevermore (a drug intended to heal faeries of iron sickness), and learns how to sword fight with a troll whose life she must save.

Booktalk: How Val went from being a typical high school girl living in the suburbs to becoming a bald-headed, much-in-need-of-a-bath Goth girl sleeping in the subway tunnels of Manhattan, and scrounging from the dumpsters for things to sell to buy food is not a pretty story. But this story does have faeries! Before you even think of Tinkerbell or other cutesy faeries, keep in mind that not all faeries are pretty and not all faeries are sweet and kind. Certainly not the faeries Val meets, those who have been exiled to the city. Angered by the realization that they are slowly being poisoned to death, they are a restless group. There is too much iron in the city for a faerie. Faeries are accustomed to living in green places, not in the gray concrete and iron jungle of New York City. Val doesn't believe in faeries, cute or otherwise, until she and her new friend Lolli break into the home of what turns out to be a troll. Told you not all faeries were cute! Ravus the troll is more than a bit upset about their intrusion into his hideaway and isn't about to let them leave easily. After seeing the wicked looking crystal sword hanging on the wall and the troll's size, Val agrees to his blackmail demands. She secures their freedom by becoming his delivery person. Val delivers Nevermore, the medicine Ravus concocts to counteract the iron sickness suffered by the faeries who are banished to the city. Both fascinated and repelled by Ravus, Val cannot help but be attracted to his Glamour side, the very good-looking young guy he changes into when he wants to go out among humans. They become friends and eventually Ravus teaches Val how to fight with the crystal sword. Will her feelings for Ravus and her newly learned sword skills be enough for her to step forward as his defender? Can she enter the Faerie Court and retrieve his still beating heart? Can she be Valiant?

Excerpt: Prologue.

Curriculum Connections: Psychology, Sociology
Have students interview other students and their families as to why they think teens run away to live on the city streets. Schedule time in the library media center for students to locate journal articles and online reports and use the data they have compiled to determine if their peers and family are accurate in their assumptions.

Similar Titles:
Bull, Emma, **Finder: A Novel of the Borderlands.** Tor, 1996, 320pp. $6.99. ISBN: 0765347776.
de Lint, Charles, **Waifs and Strays.** Viking, 2002, 304pp. $17.99. ISBN: 067003584X. Penguin, 2004, 391pp. $7.99. ISBN: 0142401587.
Farmer, Nancy, **The Sea of Trolls.** Simon & Schuster, 2006, 480pp. $17.95. ISBN: 0689867441. Simon & Schuster, 2007, 459pp. $8.99. ISBN: 0689867468. Recorded Books, 2006, $29.99. CD. ISBN: 1402593449.
Shetterly, Will, **Elsewhere.** Harcourt, 2004, 248pp. $6.95. ISBN: 0152052097.
Spiegler, Louise, **The Amethyst Road.** Houghton Mifflin, 2005, 382pp. $16. ISBN: 0618485724.

8. Blackman, Malorie, *Naughts & Crosses.*

Simon & Schuster, 2005, 386pp. $15.95. ISBN: 1416900160. Simon Pulse, 2007, 448pp. $7.99. ISBN: 1416900179.

Web Site: <www.malorieblackman.co.uk>
Subjects: Family Problems, Fathers and Daughters, Fathers and Sons, Kidnapping, Prejudices, Race Relations, Relationships, Sexual Relationships, Violence
Genres: International, Science Fiction
Levels: BL 8-11, PW 9 up, SLJ 8-10, V 7-12

Annotation: Fourteen-year-old Sephy is a Cross and the beloved daughter of an ambitious politician. Sixteen-year-old Callum is a naught and the son of a resistance fighter. Sephy and Callum grew up together because his mother was a maid. White naughts are not supposed fall in love with black Crosses, but the teens defy everyone and keep seeing each other.

Booktalk: Imagine a world where whites (naughts) were the slaves and blacks (Crosses) were the owners. Years have past and slavery no longer exists but desegregation of the schools has just begun. Blonde-haired Callum is one of the first naughts to attend his childhood friend Sephy's all Cross high school. He is very nervous as the naught schools he has attended do not have the materials the Cross schools do and he knows he is going to be placed in a lower class than the rest of his age group. History is taught a bit differently than we know it in the schools Callum and Sephy attend. For example, Henson is the Arctic explorer teachers talks about in relation to the North Pole expedition. Not Admiral Peary. History books are written with no white accomplishments listed. What would their world be like for you? How would you react to hearing about your schoolmates Sephy and Callum, a Cross and naught who have been best friends since they were in diapers, falling in love? Would you tell your parents about them? Would you turn away if you saw them together? Callum and Sephy are two young people very much in love who are caught in the fight between races and the haves and the have nots. Told they cannot love each other because of the color of their skin. Sound familiar?

Excerpt: Second paragraph on page 15 through the first line on page 19.

Curriculum Connections: English, History, Psychology
Schedule time in the library media center for students to research the history of race relations in the United States and other countries. Have students select a historical event that involved racial tension and write an essay about the event from a fictional alternative point of view, basing it on the factual information learned about the event.

Similar Titles:
Bagdasarian, Adam, *Forgotten Fire.* DK Publishing, 2000, 288pp. $19.99. ISBN: 0789426277. Random House, 2002, 304pp. $6.50. ISBN: 0440229170.
Blackman, Malorie, *Knife Edge.* Simon & Schuster, 2007, 449pp. $15.99. ISBN: 1416900187.
Frank, E.R., *Life Is Funny.* DK Publishing, 2000, 272pp. $19.99. ISBN: 078942634X. Penguin, 2002, 272pp. $7.99. ISBN: 0142300837.
Rees, Celia, *Sorceress.* Candlewick, 2002, 352pp. $15.99. ISBN: 0763618470. Candlewick, 2003, 352pp. $8.99. ISBN: 0763621838.
Woodson, Jacqueline, *If You Come Softly.* Penguin, 1998, 192pp. $16.99. ISBN: 0399231129. Penguin, 2000, 192pp. $5.99. ISBN: 0698118626.

9

Block, Francesca Lia, *Wasteland.*

HarperCollins, 2003, 160pp. $16.89. ISBN: 0060286458. HarperCollins, 2004, 150pp. $7.99. ISBN: 0064408396.

Web Site: <www.francescaliablock.com>
Subjects: Adoption, Brothers and Sisters, Emotional Problems, Grieving, Sexual Relationships, Sexuality, Suicide
Genres: Realistic
Levels: BL 9-12, KL 10 up, PW 6 up, SLJ 9 up, V 10-12

Annotation: Marina and Lex are not just siblings, they are best friends but their physical relationship takes a step too far and Lex commits suicide because of his unbrotherly feelings toward his younger sister. Told from Marina and West's point of view. West is the boy who cares and stands by her as she grieves.

Booktalk: Why is he treating me like this? We have always been more than brother and sister. We are best friends. We always have been. Who's at the beach with him every day while he surfs? Whose towel does he share? Mom says when I was born, Lex was the first person I smiled at. I had him by the heart strings when I wrapped my little baby hand around his finger. Lex is who I followed around as soon as I could walk. Lex let me follow him. He even encouraged it. We've hung out together all of our lives. At least we used to but now he doesn't want me around anymore. He pulls away from me and doesn't want me going into his room. He's dating girls from the club scene. I hate them smirking at me, with their arms around him. They are so clingy, hanging all over him. What is he doing to himself? What is he doing to us? Doesn't he understand that nothing has changed, even after what happened. That isn't going to change anything between us. I wish I could make him see that. We have nothing to be ashamed of.

Excerpt: Page 40 through page 43.

Curriculum Connections: Creative Writing, English, Psychology
West is there for Marina when Lex dies. Schedule time in the library media center for students to locate and read poetry that deals with unrequited love. Based on what they have learned from the poetry they have read and West's personality, have students write a poem that West may have written to Marina to let her know she is not alone.

Similar Titles:

Block, Francesca Lia, ***The Hanged Man.*** HarperCollins, 1999, 160pp. $8.99. ISBN: 0064408329.
Coman, Carolyn, ***Bee and Jacky.*** Front Street, 1998, 101pp. $14.95. ISBN: 1886910332. Front Street, 2006, 101pp. $9.95. ISBN: 1932425373.
Hurwin, Davida Wills, ***Circle the Soul Softly.*** HarperCollins, 2006, 176pp. $15.99. ISBN: 006077505X.

Levithan, David, ***Are We There Yet?*** Random House, 2005, 215pp. $15.95. ISBN: 037582846X.

Myers, Walter Dean, ***Autobiography of My Dead Brother.*** HarperCollins, 2005, 212pp. $15.99. ISBN: 006058291X. Amistad, 2006, 224pp. $6.99. ISBN: 0060582936.

Bowler, Tim, *Apocalypse.* — 10

Simon & Schuster, 2005, 335pp. $16.95. ISBN: 1416903704.

Web Site: <www.timbowler.co.uk>
Subjects: Accidents, Cults, Ghosts, Journeys, Kidnapping, Magic, Prejudices, Religion, Sailing, Survival, Time Travel, Violence
Genres: Adventure, Fantasy, International, Supernatural
Levels: B 10-12, KL 10-12, PW 6 up, SLJ 7 up, V 7-12

Annotation: Fifteen-year-old Kit and his parents are caught in the fog and shipwreck on a remote island inhabited by a group of religious fanatics from the past, who think Kit and his parents have been sent by the devil because Kit resembles a man the islanders fear. An orphaned girl from the past helps Kit rescue his parents.

Booktalk: Have you ever gotten the creeps, making the hair rise on your arms? That's how I responded to many of the situations in this book. Like when Kit is behind the wheel of his family's small sailboat as they enter a fog bank and a hand rises out of the water and hands him a tiny wooden boat. How is that possible? But there it is—a little wooden sailboat at his feet. There couldn't have been a man coming up out of the water to hand him the boat, but there he was. Before Kit could refocus on sailing through the fog, their sailboat crashes into a large rock. They are just able to sail the damaged boat close to the shore of a nearby island. At first the remote island appears uninhabited, but Kit's family soon discovers that there is a fanatical religious group living on the other side of the island. Things get even weirder when the villagers think Kit and his parents are a danger to them. Then Kit's parents disappear and their sailboat is sunk. Kit is sure it was the villagers who kidnapped or killed his parents and he heads across the island to confront them. Who he finds on his trek across the island will stop him in his tracks. She claims the wooden sailboat is hers and that she is from the past and she needs his help. When all the violence is over, who actually helped who?

Excerpt: Page 107 through the first paragraph on page 110.

Curriculum Connections: Geography, History, Science
The Cairn Islanders knew to retreat to higher ground when the tidal wave came. Schedule time in the library media center for students to research tidal wave activity in the various island regions of the world and how the indigenous people adapted to the possibility of a tidal wave and the aftermath of a tidal wave.

Similar Titles:
Bowler, Tim, ***River Boy.*** Simon & Schuster, 2002, 234pp. $4.99. ISBN: 0689848048. Chivers Audio Books, 2001, $34.95. CD. ISBN: 0754065030.
Cooney, Caroline B., ***Wanted!*** Scholastic, 1997, 240pp. $5.99. ISBN: 0590988492.
Duncan, Lois, ***The Third Eye.*** Random House, 1985, 224pp. $5.99. ISBN: 0440987202.
L'Engle, Madeleine, ***Many Waters.*** Farrar, Straus & Giroux, 1986, 310pp. $18. ISBN: 0374347964. Random House, 1998, 310pp. $5.99. ISBN: 0440227704.
Westerfeld, Scott, ***Blue Noon.*** HarperCollins, 2006, 378pp. $15.95. ISBN: 0060519576.

11. Brashares, Ann, *Sisterhood of the Traveling Pants.*

Random House, 2001, 320pp. $15.95. ISBN: 0385729332. Random House, 2003, 336pp. $8.95. ISBN: 0385730586. Listening Library, 2001, $26. ISBN: 0807205893. Random House, 2005, $30. CD. ISBN: 0307243273.

Subjects: Body Image, Cancer, Family Problems, Friendship, Grandparents, Journeys, Letter Writing, Sexual Relationships, Stepfamilies, Summer Camps
Genres: Humor, Realistic, Sports
Levels: PW 6 up, SLJ 9 up, V 7-12

Annotation: Four best friends, 15-year-old Tibby, Bridget, Lena, and Carmen find a pair of jeans at a second hand store that fits all four of them perfectly, even though their body forms are very different. They send the pants and letters to each other while they spend the summer apart, finding out more about themselves and their families.

Booktalk: How could I resist him? He was gorgeous! I decided that he was the guy I wanted and I went after him. I know that this is soccer camp, not time for a summer romance. It started out with me challenging him to a race when we were out jogging. I beat him, of course. I have always wanted to be first at everything. The best. And, most of the time I am. I don't brag but I am pretty confident about my physical abilities. The soccer field is my world and I should have left it at that. But he was so cute and I was so hung up on him that I chased him. I teased and taunted him and showed up at places the players weren't supposed to go, including a bar where the coaches hang out. I knew I was going well beyond what I should have in relation to this guy. He was a college guy, but like everything else in my life, when I want something I go after it. He didn't stand a chance. I chased him until he caught me, just like I wanted. How could he not? I went to his cabin in the middle of the night. Now I am curled up in my cot crying. Sometimes what you get is not what you need or are ready for.

Excerpt: From break on page 165 through page 168.

Curriculum Connections: English, Foreign Languages
Lena goes to Greece for the summer to stay with her grandparents. Her grandfather does not speak English, as is the case with most of the Greeks she is around. Schedule time in the library media center for students to use a variety of foreign language dictionaries to translate a short section of dialogue from the novel. Have them discuss as a group the similarities among the languages.

Similar Titles:
Brashares, Ann, *Forever in Blue: Fourth Summer of the Sisterhood.* Delacorte, 2007, 240pp. $18.99. ISBN: 0385729367.
Brashares, Ann, *Girls in Pants: Third Summer of the Sisterhood.* Bantam Doubleday Dell, 2005, 352pp. $16.95. ISBN: 0385729359. Delacorte, 2006, 368pp. $8.95. ISBN: 0553375938. Listening Library, 2005, $34. ISBN: 1400099439.
Brashares, Ann, *The Second Summer of the Sisterhood.* Delacorte, 2003, 373pp. $15.95. ISBN: 0385729340. Delacorte, 2004, 416pp. $8.95. ISBN: 0385731051. Listening Library, 2003, $30. ISBN: 080721969X. Random House Audio, 2004, $55. CD. ISBN: 0807216151.
Dessen, Sarah, *Just Listen.* Viking, 2006, 384pp. $17.99. ISBN: 0670061050.
Lockhart, E., *The Boyfriend List: 15 Guys, 11 Shrink Appointments, 4 Ceramic Frogs, and Me, Ruby Oliver.* Random House, 2005, 240pp. $15.95. ISBN: 0385732066. Delacorte, 2006, 256pp. $8.95. ISBN: 0385732074. Listening Library, 2005, $30. ISBN: 1400099455.

Bray, Libba, *A Great and Terrible Beauty.*

12

Bantam Doubleday Dell, 2003, 416pp. $16.95. ISBN: 0385730284. Delacorte, 2005, 403pp. $8.95. ISBN: 0385732317. Random House Audio, 2004, $30. ISBN: 0807220665. Random House Audio, 2004, $60. CD. ISBN: 1400086213.

Web Site: <www.libbabray.com>
Subjects: Boarding Schools, Friendship, Ghosts, Grieving, Gypsies, Magic, Mothers and Daughters, Prejudices, Teachers, Time Travel
Genres: Fantasy, Historical, International, Supernatural
Lists: 2004 BBYA
Levels: BL 8-12, KL 10-12, PW 6 up, SLJ 9 up, V 10-12

Annotation: When 16-year-old Gemma's mother dies in 1895, she leaves India to attend the English boarding school her mother had attended and discovers she has magical powers that allow her, and her friends, to enter a mysterious realm where their wishes come true, but holds a truth for Gemma she doesn't want to believe.

Booktalk: The last day we were together in Bombay I was not very nice to my mother. I complained about being with her in the market instead of being in school in London like most girls of sixteen. Now that I am, indeed, in the very same boarding school my mother attended, I wish I had been nicer to Mother. If so, maybe I wouldn't be here. I don't fit in with these snobbish girls who talk about me behind their gloved hands. That day in the market, I had no idea it would be the last day I would ever spend with my mother. I was complaining about India being rotten from the inside out, just like the over ripe dates in the market, as the man in the white turban ran into my mother. When he stopped to apologize I saw the panic on my mother's face. She recognized him and he scared her. I asked her what was wrong but she became angry and told me I vexed her. Her look made it very clear that I was an embarrassment and a disappointment to her. Responding to the hurt look on my face, she realized how cold her words were. She tried to make up for her harshness by removing from her own neck, and putting around mine, the necklace of hers that I had always wanted. I wasn't about to be bribed and I said the worst thing I could think of to say to her at the time because she was sending me home without telling me where she was going. When I asked to accompany her she said no and that she would be home shortly. I was just as vexed as she and told her that I didn't care if she came home at all. She didn't, at least not alive.

Excerpt: From break on page 99 to break on page 104.

Curriculum Connections: Art, English

The art teacher asks the girls at Spencer Academy to compare the words of Tennyson's poem "The Lady of Shallot" with a sketch she made based on the poem. Schedule time in the library media center for students to select a poem from which to create a sketch that visually represents the central theme of the poem.

Similar Titles:

Boylan, Clare, **Emma Brown**. Viking, 2004, 448pp. $25.95. ISBN: 0307280675. Penguin, 2005, 464pp. $14. ISBN: 0143034839.

Bray, Libba, **Rebel Angels.** Delacorte, 2005, 560pp. ISBN: 1416900187. Delacorte, 2005, 592pp. $9.99. ISBN: 0385733410. Listening Library, 2005, $50. ISBN: 0307280675.

McGhee, Alison, **Shadow Baby.** Picador, 2003, 256pp. $14. ISBN: 0312423772.

Stevermer, Caroline, **A College of Magics.** Starscape, 2002, 480pp. $5.99. ISBN: 0765342456.

Wrede, Patricia C., **Sorcery and Cecelia or the Enchanted Chocolate Pot: Being the Correspondence of Two Young Ladies of Quality Regarding Various Magical Scandals in London and the Country.** Harcourt, 2003, 336pp. $17. ISBN: 0152046151. Magic Carpet, 2004, 336pp. $6.95. ISBN: 015205300X.

Brooks, Bruce, *Dolores: Seven Stories About Her.*
HarperCollins, 2002, 135pp. $15.89. ISBN: 0060294736. HarperCollins, 2003, 144pp. $6.99. ISBN: 0060540621.

Subjects: Brothers and Sisters, Divorce, Kidnapping, Self-Esteem
Genres: Realistic
Levels: BL 8-12, K 5 up, PW 6 up, SLJ 7-10, V 7-12

Annotation: Dolores is a feisty female, from her almost abduction at age 7, to surviving malicious 7th grade rumors, to playing hockey on an all boys team, to becoming an unorthodox football cheerleader, and at age 16, saving herself from yet another attempted abduction.

Booktalk: How can you not like a little kid who can sing along to Nirvana? At age 7, Do, short for Dolores, was already into heavy metal music and could sing along with the lyrics. Her older brother Jimmy tried to look out for Do but she was an independent soul, even as a little kid. She has always had a calm demeanor, no matter what was happening. For example, 7-year-old Do was in the process of being kidnapped from the Wal-Mart where Jimmy worked. There she was, calmly sitting on the toilet letting the women dye her hair black when Jimmy came charging in and finds them. Do calmly tells her big brother, "I'm getting what you call a makeover." Deep inside Do might have been scared silly, but she wasn't about to let anyone know that. This is just the first of Do's escapades over the next 10 years. She held her own as a hockey player on an all boys traveling team. When she decides to become a cheerleader, it was because she liked to scream, not because she wanted to impress some guy on the team. Don't miss her last escapade. It might feel just like a kick in the stomach, literally.

Excerpt: Second to last paragraph on page 24 through page 28.

Curriculum Connections: Physical Education
Schedule time in the library media center for students to research women in male-dominated sports. Based on their research, have students discuss the sports in which changes have occurred, such as the recent popularity of women's soccer and women playing softball during WWII.

Similar Titles:
Bauer, Joan, *Hope Was Here.* Putnam, 2000, 192pp. $16.99. ISBN: 0399231420. Putnam, 2002, 192pp. $5.99. ISBN: 0698119517. Random House Audio, 2003, $25. ISBN: 0807216976.
Creech, Sharon, *The Wanderer.* HarperCollins, 1999, 320pp. $16.89. ISBN: 0060277319. HarperCollins, 2002, 320pp. $5.99. ISBN: 0064410323. Random House Audio, 2000, $25. ISBN: 080728243X.
Naylor, Phyllis Reynolds, *Including Alice.* Simon & Schuster, 2004, 277pp. $15.95. ISBN: 0689826370.

Spinelli, Jerry, **Stargirl.** Knopf, 2000, 192pp. $17.99. ISBN: 0679986375. Random House, 2004, 208pp. $6.99. ISBN: 0440416779. Random House Audio, 2001, $25. ISBN: 0807205710.

Voigt, Cynthia, **Dicey's Song.** Atheneum, 1982, 204pp. $17.95. ISBN: 0689309449. Simon Pulse, 2002, 368pp. $6.99. ISBN: 0689851316. Bantam Books Audio, 1997, $19.99. ISBN: 0553478230.

14 Brooks, Kevin, *Candy.*

Scholastic, 2005, 364pp. $16.95. ISBN: 0439683270. Scholastic, 2006, 368pp. $7.99. ISBN: 0439683289.

Subjects: Brothers and Sisters, Cities, Drug Abuse, Music, Prostitution, Relationships, Runaways, Violence
Genres: International, Realistic
Levels: BL 9-12, PW 6 up, SLJ 9 up

Annotation: Joe, a quiet 15-year-old musician, falls for Candy, a drug-addicted runaway who sells her body to stay alive on the streets of London. Joe risks his life to help her get away from prostitution and drugs.

Booktalk: How could I resist? He was just so adorable—clean cut and cute with his hat and all. I was slouched against the wall waiting to pick up someone when I saw him get off the train. He looked so innocent. So unlike me. I haven't been innocent in so long I don't even remember how to spell it. I couldn't resist him even though I knew I would be in big trouble with Iggy for getting involved with anyone who wasn't paying for my attention, especially a teenage guy who didn't even know what I was. We ended up at McDonalds. We looked like any teenage couple out for a bite to eat in London. Well, at first that's the way it looked. Then they came and sat in the next booth. I knew who they were right away, but this Joe guy didn't. He just kept looking at me like I wasn't real. Like I really was a piece of candy—the name I use on the streets. He had no idea what was going on when they told him to stay away from me. But I could see from the look in his eyes that he wasn't going to stay away. And I knew from the way he made me feel that I wasn't going to let him stay away. He made me feel not quite as hollow inside or as alone as I normally do. But this isn't my story. It's Joe's story. Joe's story of how he saved me, Candy.

Excerpt: From the break on page 189 through "I may as well hate myself, too." on page 191.

Curriculum Connections: Health, Psychology, Science
Schedule time in the library media center for students to research the historical and modern theories about addiction. Have students discuss what they have learned and

brainstorm the different things a person can become addicted to, addressing how even an addiction to a good thing can be dangerous.

Similar Titles:
Anonymous, **Go Ask Alice.** Simon & Schuster, 1971, 159pp. $16.95. ISBN: 0671664581. Simon & Schuster, 2005, 224pp. $6.99. ISBN: 1416914633.
Brooks, Kevin, **Martyn Pig.** Scholastic, 2002, 240pp. $16.95. ISBN: 0439295955. Scholastic, 2003, 233pp. $6.99. ISBN: 0439507529.
Going, K.L., **Fat Kid Rules the World.** Penguin, 2003, 192pp. $17.99. ISBN: 0399239901. Penguin, 2004, 192pp. $6.99. ISBN: 0142402087.
Qualey, Marsha, **One Night.** Dial, 2002, 176pp. $16.99. ISBN: 0803726023. Penguin, 2003, 176pp. $5.99. ISBN: 0142501506.
Rapp, Adam, **Under the Wolf, Under the Dog.** Candlewick, 2004, 210pp. $16.99. ISBN: 0763618187.

Brooks, Kevin, *Lucas: A Story of Love and Hate.*
Scholastic, 2003, 423pp. $16.95. ISBN: 0439456983. Scholastic, 2004, 384pp. $7.99. ISBN: 0439530636.

Subjects: Alcoholism, Brothers and Sisters, Fathers and Daughters, Gangs, Murder, Peer Pressure, Prejudices, Runaways, Violence, Writing
Genres: International, Realistic, Suspense
Lists: 2004 BBYA
Levels: BL 8-10, KL 7-12, PW 7 up, SLJ 9 up, V 7-12

Annotation: Fifteen-year-old Caitlin, disgusted by the behavior of her brother and his rowdy friends, is drawn to Lucas, the quiet blonde-haired boy who shows up on their remote British island. The locals don't understand Lucas and accuse him of a violent crime.

Booktalk: Have you ever seen someone that you felt you just had to meet? That's the way I felt about Lucas. I saw him walking on the beach and I knew he was someone I wanted to get to know. I live on a small island and we all know each other and our secrets. Everyone knows my dad is a writer and that he drinks too much. They all know about my brother and his gang of rowdy friends. And they all know I keep to myself but this is one time I went out of my way to meet someone. I kept thinking about him and wondering who he was and why he was on our island. I even dreamt about him, but it wasn't a good dream. I dreamt that people were chasing him on the beach and calling him names. I was down on the beach with Deefer, my dog, when I saw him. He was standing barefoot by a tide pool and held a crab in one hand and a length of twine in the other. He flung the twine with a piece of meat tied to the end back into the pool before he turned to me, smiled, and said hello. That's when I officially met Lucas. He knew my name. One of the islanders had already told him who I was. I liked the slow way he moved and the way he didn't scare me or make me nervous like the other boys on the island did. I sat down next to the water and we began to talk. It was right then and there that I fell in love with Lucas. Looking back I'd like to say I wish I hadn't, but even after what happened to him on my island I'm still glad I met and loved Lucas.

Excerpt: Page 7 through page 10.

Curriculum Connections: Science

Swamps and tidal flats may include areas that a person can sink into and drown or suffocate. Schedule time in the library media center for students to research what geologically must be present for sink holes in swamps or marshes to occur. Have students brainstorm a list of clues that could help someone avoid these areas.

Similar Titles:

Bagdasarian, Adam, ***First French Kiss: And Other Traumas.*** Farrar, Straus & Giroux, 2002, 144pp. $16. ISBN: 0374323380. Farrar, Straus & Giroux, 2005, 144pp. $5.99. ISBN: 0374423237.

Cole, Brock, ***The Goats.*** Farrar, Straus & Giroux, 1990, 184pp. $6.95. ISBN: 0374425752.

Koertge, Ron, ***Stoner and Spaz.*** Candlewick, 2002, 176pp. $15.99. ISBN: 0763616087. Candlewick, 2003, 176pp. $6.99. ISBN: 0763621501. Listening Library, 2003, $18. ISBN: 0807212458.

Lawrence, Iain, ***The Lightkeeper's Daughter.*** Bantam Doubleday Dell, 2002, 256pp. $16.95. ISBN: 0385729251. Delacorte, 2004, 272pp. $7.95. ISBN: 0385731272.

Plum-Ucci, Carol, ***What Happened to Lani Garner?*** Harcourt, 2002, 328pp. $17. ISBN: 0152168133. Harcourt, 2004, 336pp. $6.95. ISBN: 0152050884.

16 Brooks, Kevin, *The Road of the Dead.*

Scholastic, 2006, 339pp. $16.99. ISBN: 0439786231. Scholastic Push, 2007, 368pp. $7.99. ISBN: 043978624X.

Subjects: Brothers, Brothers and Sisters, Crime, Death, Gypsies, Journeys, Murder, Prejudices, Rape, Violence

Genres: International, Mystery, Realistic, Suspense

Lists: BBYA 2006

Levels: BL 9-12, PW 7 up, SLJ 9 up, V 5-12

Annotation: Fourteen-year-old Ruben inherited the sight from his father's Gypsy side of the family. He and his older brother, 17-year-old Cole, travel from London to the isolated northern moors to find their 19-year-old sister's murderer so they can bring her body home. They are helped by the Gypsies who know their father.

Booktalk: Ruben is the calm and quiet one in the family, especially since their father, a Gypsy, was put in prison for killing a guy during a "fixed" fight. Ruben's older brother Cole has his own kind of quiet. It is the same kind of menacing quiet that their father has. Sometimes their kind of quietness scares Ruben, but he knows that when something has to be done, Cole can turn off his heart and do it. And now is one of those times. Their older sister Rachel has been raped, beaten, and murdered in the moors while walking back to her friend's house. The police will not release Rachel's body until the murderer is apprehended. Their mother's grief and her need to bury her only daughter are the reasons why Cole is headed to the moors to find the killer so they can put Rachel to rest. Ruben is going with Cole, whether he likes it or not, because Ruben has promised his mother he will look after his volatile older brother. They also know that Ruben has the sight, which will help them locate the killer. What they don't know is that Ruben heard Rachel call to him the night she was murdered. He can still smell the Dead Man just as he did in his dream. He was with his older sister when the Dead Man took her down to the earth. Ruben wants to be with Cole when they find their sister's killer, but Ruben also fears the encounter as he knows who murdered his sister is no normal man.

Excerpt: From the first break on page 10 to the break on page 15.

Curriculum Connections: History, Sociology
Schedule time in the library media center for students to research Gypsies, sometimes called Travelers, to determine the reasons for their nomadic lifestyle and why some people react negatively to them.

Similar Titles:
Cheripko, Jan, **Sun Moon Stars Rain.** Front Street, 2005, 160pp. $16.95. ISBN: 1932425535.
Cormier, Robert, **Heroes.** Random House, 2000, 144pp. $5.99. ISBN: 0440227690.
Glass, Linzi, **The Year the Gypsies Came.** Holt, 2006, 260pp. $16.95. ISBN: 0805079998.
Pearson, Mary E., **Scribbler of Dreams.** Harcourt, 2001, 240pp. $17. ISBN: 0152023208.
Rottman, S.L., **Shadow of a Doubt.** Peachtree, 2003, 224pp. $14.95. ISBN: 1561452912. Peachtree, 2005, 197pp. $7.95. ISBN: 1561453544.

17 Brooks, Martha, *True Confessions of a Heartless Girl.*

Farrar, Straus & Giroux, 2003, 181pp. $16. ISBN: 0374378061. HarperTempest, 2004, 216pp. $6.99. ISBN: 0060594977.

Subjects: Emotional Problems, Journeys, Mothers and Daughters, Pregnancy, Runaways, Self-Esteem, Sexual Relationships, Sisters, Theft
Genres: International, Realistic
Lists: 2004 BBYA
Levels: BL 9-12, KL 7-12, PW 9 up, SLJ 9 up

Annotation: Seventeen-year-old Noreen runs away from home, becomes pregnant while living with a young Native man who picked her up while she's hitchhiking, steals his truck, and finds herself in a small Canadian prairie town where the local people accept her.

Booktalk: Have any of you felt like no matter what you did it turned out wrong? I see lots of you nodding your heads and grimacing. That's what happens to Noreen. It isn't like she is the perfect person. Matter of fact, she has a real attitude, but she has it for good reason. Her mom married a guy who was supposed to take care of her and her little girl, but it sure didn't turn out that way. Gladys, Noreen's older stepsister, pretty much raised Noreen, but when Gladys got married, Noreen careened out of control. She ran away and got mixed up with the guy who picked her up hitchhiking. But she runs away from him too and ends up in a tiny prairie town with bad luck biting at her heels. Noreen proceeds to send a little boy's dog to the vet, set fire to a grieving man's photographs of his dead brother, and pull down a wall in the only restaurant in town. You'd think after all that the residents would drive her to the edge of town and drop her off, or put her on the next bus. Instead, Seth, the boy with the dog; Del, the man who lost his brother; and Lynda, the restaurant owner, along with two little old ladies, gently force Noreen to take responsibility for her "accidents" and help this "heartless girl" realize she's not so heartless after all.

Excerpt: First chapter.

Curriculum Connections: Creative Writing, Drama, English
Del has been grieving his brother's death for a long time. Schedule time in the library media center for students to locate plays and become familiar with how they are written and formatted. Have students work in pairs to write and present a script style dialog they think Del would have had with his brother after Noreen burned his chair.

Similar Titles:
Dessen, Sarah, *Someone Like You.* Viking, 1998, 281pp. $16.99. ISBN: 0670877786. Penguin, 2004, 281pp. $7.99. ISBN: 0142401773. Listening Library, 2003, $26. ISBN: 0807215643.

Howard-Barr, Elissa, ***The Truth About Sexual Behavior and Unplanned Pregnancy.*** Facts on File, 2005, 192pp. $35. ISBN: 0816053073.
Hrdlitschka, Shelley, ***Dancing Naked.*** Orca, 2002, 240pp. $6.95. ISBN: 1551432102.
Pennebaker, Ruth, ***Don't Think Twice.*** Holt, 2001, 272pp. $7.95. ISBN: 0805067299.
Woodson, Jacqueline, ***The Dear One.*** Penguin, 2004, 128pp. $17.99. ISBN: 0399239685. Penguin, 2004, 144pp. $6.99. ISBN: 0142501905.

Burnham, Niki, *Sticky Fingers.*

Simon Pulse, 2005, 278pp. $6.99. ISBN: 0689876491.

Web Site: <www.nikiburnham.com>
Subjects: Friendship, High Schools, Peer Pressure, Relationships, Sexual Assault, Sexuality, Stress, Testing, Theft, Universities and Colleges
Genres: Realistic
Levels: BL 9-12, SLJ 7 up

Annotation: Jenna, a goal-directed high school senior, received early acceptance into Harvard, so now her boyfriend Jeff thinks it is time for her to forget about school and studying and relax enough to have sex with him so he gives her a date rape drug.

Booktalk: I like the cover of this book. It shows a girl's arms around a guy in a white t-shirt and blue jeans. But all you see is from their knees to their necks. Who are these two? Piqued my interest. Once I started reading it I began to relate to the main character Jenna because she's an A student, but one who has to work really hard for her grades. Those As only come after many hours of studying and doing homework. Her boyfriend Scott, on the other hand, is the good-looking jock who aces the tests without studying and can't figure out why Jenna doesn't just chill and party with him. Jenna cannot help but stress about grades and school. She is intent on going to college. Life should have gotten easier for Jenna when she earned early admittance to Harvard, but it didn't. Sliding by is not her style but Scott is insistent that she relax. He has other things on his mind than hitting the books. He thinks it's time for Jenna to focus on him and take their relationship to the next step. Go beyond just steaming up the windows in his Jetta. With Scott pressuring her to go farther than she is ready to, Jenna is now unsure about her feelings for him. She has no one to talk to about what's happening because her best friend Courtney is acting really strange. Scott takes things way too far and Courtney plays a role in what happens to Jenna.

Excerpt: Page 17 through page 21.

Curriculum Connections: Biology, Health

Jenna is given a date rape drug. Schedule time in the library media center for students to research the ingredients in the various date rape drugs and how they affect a person's ability to function normally. With this knowledge, have students discuss how they can safeguard themselves against these drugs.

Similar Titles:

Anderson, Laurie Halse, *Catalyst.* Viking, 2002, 240pp. $17.99. ISBN: 0670035661. Puffin, 2003, 240pp. $6.99. ISBN: 0142400017. Listening Library, 2002, $26. ISBN: 0807209392.
Bode, Janet, *Voices of Rape.* Scholastic, 1998, 160pp. $24. ISBN: 0531115186. Scholastic, 1999, 160pp. $9.95. ISBN: 0531159329.
Landau, Elaine, *Date Violence.* Scholastic, 2004, 80pp. $20.50. ISBN: 053112214X. Franklin Watts, 2005, 80pp. $6.95. ISBN: 0531166139.
Lynch, Chris, *Inexcusable.* Simon & Schuster, 2005, 165pp. $16.95. ISBN: 0689847890.
Pollack, Jenny, *Klepto.* Penguin, 2006, 288pp. $16.99. ISBN: 0670060615.

19 Charlton-Trujillo, e.E., *Feels Like Home.*
Delacorte, 2007, 209pp. $17.99. ISBN: 0385733321.

Web Site: <www.bigdreamswrite.com>
Subjects: Alcoholism, Brothers and Sisters, Death, Fires, Football, Friendship, Grieving, High Schools, Hispanics, Peer Pressure, Prejudices, Race Relations, Relationships, Self-Esteem, Stress, Universities and Colleges
Genres: Multicultural, Realistic
Levels: LMC 9-12, PW 6 up

Annotation: Seventeen-year-old Mickey's brother returns to their small Texas border town when their father dies, but Mickey isn't ready to forgive him for leaving her behind with their alcoholic father after the fire at the football stadium that killed his best friend.

Booktalk: I can't believe he actually showed up. How dare he do this to me after all these years? I finally got over him leaving me behind. Not a word from him for six years after the fire and then he just shows up at Dad's funeral. He left me behind to deal with all the whispers and all the angry parents who were sure Roland would have been the first Mexican-American football player to make it into the NFL. All the whispers that Roland wouldn't be dead if it weren't for him. I got over it and I really didn't need any friends, but Christina insisted on being friends even though her mom doesn't want her hanging out with a weird gringa. But even if I didn't have a friend in the world, I still wouldn't need him. He can just get back on the bus, or however else he got here, and go back to wherever it is he came from. I don't care! I really don't care. And I'm going to take that dumb book about Ponyboy and Sodapop and all about staying golden and I am going to throw it at his feet. Who says I need a big brother? I don't. I swear I don't.

Excerpt: Page 43 through the ninth paragraph on page 46.

Curriculum Connections: Creative Writing, English
Danny read S.E. Hinton's *The Outsiders* to Mickey when she was a young girl. Schedule time in the library media center for students to read reviews and other information about the characters in *The Outsiders*. Have students choose a character from the book, such as Ponyboy or Darry, and write him a letter from Mickey's perspective, sharing how she felt about her brother leaving her behind.

Similar Titles:
Dean, Carolee, ***Comfort.*** Houghton Mifflin, 2002, 240pp. $15. ISBN: 0618138463.
Draper, Sharon M., ***Forged by Fire.*** Hazelwood High Trilogy. Simon & Schuster, 1998, 160pp. $5.99. ISBN: 0689818513.
Hinton, S.E., ***The Outsiders.*** Viking, 1967, 192pp. $17.99. ISBN: 0670532576. Puffin, 2006, 208pp. $10. ISBN: 014240733X. Random House Audio, 2006. $25. CD. ISBN: 073933901X.
Lowry, Brigid, ***Follow the Blue.*** Holiday House, 2004, 205pp. $16.95. ISBN: 0823418278. St. Martin's Press, 2006, 208pp. $8.95. ISBN: 0312342977.
Rice, David Talbot, ***Crazy Loco.*** Puffin, 2003, 144pp. $5.99. ISBN: 0142500569.

Chotjewitz, David, *Daniel Half Human and the Good Nazi.* | 20

Atheneum, 2004, 304pp. $17.95. ISBN: 0689857470. Simon & Schuster, 2006, 336pp. $5.99. ISBN: 0689857489.

Subjects: Bullying, Fathers and Sons, Friendship, Jews, Mothers and Sons, Peer Pressure, Prejudices, Race Relations, Religion, Stress, Teachers, Violence, War
Genres: Historical, International
Lists: 2005 BBYA
Levels: BL 7-12, PW 7 up, SLJ 7 up

Annotation: Daniel's desire to be part of the Hitler Youth in 1933 changes when he learns his mother is Jewish and he has to rethink his place in the world and who his friends are after his best friend becomes a Nazi soldier. The perspective alternates between Daniel as a young adult before the war and later as a translator for the U.S. Army.

Booktalk: We often read about how horrible the Nazis were, but we rarely read about a teenager who wanted to join Hitler's Youth. This is the case with young Daniel. He and his friend Armin play Nazis all the time. They dream of joining Hitler's Youth. They revel in the stories Daniel's father tells of his time in the German Army. Because his father had been a soldier in World War I Daniel cannot understand why he gets so upset whenever Daniel talks about joining the Hitler Youth. Daniel's angry outbursts do no good. Rather than explaining his adamant refusal of Daniel's demands to join the Hitler Youth, his father sends him to his room. When these altercations occur between father and son, Daniel's mother becomes very quiet and walks away. Daniel is persistent and keeps asking why he cannot join, long after Armin's father allows his own son to join. It isn't until the acts against the Jews become more violent that the truth about his mother is shared with Daniel. A truth that means no matter how much he feels like a member of the Aryan German race, he cannot join the Hitler Youth. The Nazis now consider him half human.

Excerpt: First paragraph on page 10 through page 13.

Curriculum Connections: History
Schedule a time in the library media center for students to research the Hitler Youth and discuss who joined this group as well as the membership requirements in relation to why Daniel could not join.

Similar Titles:
Cartlidge, Cherese, *Life of a Nazi Soldier.* Thomson Gale, 2000, 96pp. $27.80. ISBN: 1560064846.
Dvorson, Alexa, *The Hitler Youth: Marching Toward Madness.* Rosen, 1999, 64pp. $17.95. ISBN: 0823927830.
Kater, Michael H., *Hitler Youth.* Harvard University Press, 2004, 368pp. $27.95. ISBN: 0674014960. Harvard University Press, 2006, 368pp. $16.95. ISBN: 0674019911.
Spinelli, Jerry, *Milkweed.* Knopf, 2003, 223pp. $15.95. ISBN: 0375813748. Random House, 2005, 240pp. $6.50. ISBN: 0440420059. Listening Library, 2003, $25. ISBN: 0807218588.
Wulffson, Don, *Soldier X.* Penguin, 2003, 240pp. $6.99. ISBN: 0142500739.

21 Cirrone, Dorian, *Dancing in Red Shoes Will Kill You.*

HarperCollins, 2005, 224pp. $15.99. ISBN: 006055701X. HarperCollins, 2005, 224pp. $7.99. ISBN: 0060557036.

Web Site: <www.doriancirrone.com>
Subjects: Art, Ballet, Body Image, Dancing, Occupations, Peer Pressure, Prejudices, Relationships, Self-Esteem, Sisters, Stress, Teachers, Theft
Genres: Humor, Mystery, Realistic
Levels: BL 9-12, KL 10-12, PW 7 up, SLJ 7-10

Annotation: Kayla, a junior at a private arts school, is a talented dancer but is passed over for the lead in the school's ballet of Cinderella. She does not have the willowy stereotypical body type of a ballerina because she is very large breasted. Kayla is further ostracized by some members of the dance group when the lead ballerina is threatened and Kayla, cast as a wicked stepsister, becomes the prime suspect.

Booktalk: Kayla has a wicked sense of humor—something that is required when you are a ballerina with double Ds. She says "even NASA couldn't design a tank suit to camouflage my proportions." Kayla hadn't considered the possibility of being anything other than what and who she is until she is passed up for the lead role in Cinderella because of her breasts. They would be a distraction says the visiting director. That would be Timm with two m's. Not one of Kayla's favorite people in the world of ballet at the moment. When Kayla asks for advice, her ballet teacher suggests she see a plastic surgeon about breast reduction if she wants to continue her pursuit of becoming a ballerina. Kayla considers it, but she doesn't like the idea of changing her body. She likes who she is and so does her new boyfriend Gray who is supportive of her decision against surgery. The other guys in school seem to be obsessed with her chest size, even to the point of wearing "save the hooters" pins when they hear about her possible reduction surgery, but Gray is not. Kayla has more than her body to worry about as opening day draws nearer. Rumor has it that she is out to get the dancer chosen to play Cinderella. Kayla has not made it a secret that she doesn't like her, but Kayla isn't the type to seek revenge. But with Kayla cast in the part of the wicked stepsister who wears red dance slippers and with someone leaving a pair of them hanging on the lead ballerina's door, everyone figures the threat had to come from Kayla. We know it isn't Kayla, so who is threatening Cinderella?

Excerpt: Page 4 through page 8.

Curriculum Connections: Health, Physical Education
Schedule time in the library media center for students to research a sport they feel requires a specific body type, such a gymnastics, figure skating, or basketball. Based on their research, have students work as a group to create a list of physical attributes that typify an athlete in each sport.

Similar Titles:
Dowd, Olympia, *A Young Dancer's Apprenticeship.* Learner, 2004, 128pp. $24.90. ISBN: 076132917X.
Freymann-Weyr, Garret, *The Kings Are Already Here.* Houghton Mifflin, 2003, 160pp. $15. ISBN: 0618263632. Penguin, 2004, 160pp. $6.99. ISBN: 0142402079.
Hewett, Lorri, *Dancer: Everyone Has a Dream.* Penguin, 2001, 224pp. $5.99. ISBN: 0141310855.
Mackler, Carolyn, *The Earth, My Butt, and Other Big Round Things*. Candlewick, 2003, 246pp. $15.99. ISBN: 0763619582. Candlewick, 2005, 256pp. $8.99. ISBN: 0763620912.
Rinaldi, Robin, *Ballet.* Chelsea House, 2004, 120pp. $22.95. ISBN: 0791076407.

22 Cohn, Rachel, *Pop Princess.*

Simon & Schuster, 2004, 311pp. $16.95. ISBN: 0689852053. Simon Pulse, 2005, 311pp. $6.99. ISBN: 1416902635.

Web Site: <www.rachelcohn.com>
Subjects: Accidents, Body Image, Cities, Dancing, Friendship, Jealousy, Music, Occupations, Self-Esteem, Sisters, Weight Control
Genres: Realistic
Levels: BL 8-12, KL 7-12, PW 8 up, SLJ 8 up

Annotation: Fifteen-year-old Wonder Blake realizes that being a pop princess is not what she wants out of her musical career after she is recruited as an opening act for Kayla, a friend of Wonder's dead older sister, and is indoctrinated into Kayla's self-centered world of excesses.

Booktalk: I thought being a pop star would be so different from my prior life as the unpopular girl at school and the forgettable younger sister of Lucky, the beloved young singer who died. My family was falling apart so I was enjoying my time away from home while I worked at the local Dairy Queen. That's where I was when I was "discovered." I had my headphones on, mopping the floor, and singing along with a CD when my sister's manager heard me and offered a record contract on the spot. As soon as I accepted, one of the singers in Lucky's old group, Kayla, now a pop star on her own, shows up to help get me physically and emotionally ready to go on stage. Since Lucky died I had been eating a bit too much and wasn't as thin as pop stars are supposed to be so I had my work cut out for me. But all the dieting and exercise were worth it when I stepped out onto the stage for the first time. I felt at home with the microphone in my hand. Pretty soon my life was filled with concerts, late nights at clubs with Kayla, and closets full of clothes and shoes. The perfect life of a teen star. I thought so, at least at first. Then I realized Kayla was stabbing me in the back. She was worried I was taking too much of the attention away from her. And the guy I was nuts about was into Kayla, not me. Even though she didn't like him, she was going to give him just enough attention so he didn't see me at all. Maybe it's time I go home. High school and the Dairy Queen don't look so bad from up here on stage with Kayla glaring at me.

Excerpt: Page 86 through page 89.

Curriculum Connections: Career Education, Psychology, Sociology

Schedule time in the library media center for students to research teenage pop stars of the Eighties and Nineties to determine how long they were singers and what they are doing now. Discuss what is different about the lives of the singers who are still involved professionally compared to those who are not.

Similar Titles:
Manning, Sarra, ***Guitar Girl.*** Dutton, 2004, 224pp. $15.99. ISBN: 0525472347. Puffin, 2005, 240pp. $6.99. ISBN: 0142403180.
Mayer, Melody, ***The Nannies.*** Bantam Doubleday Dell, 2005, 288pp. $10.99. ISBN: 0385903006. Bantam Doubleday Dell, 2005, 288pp. $8.95. ISBN: 038573283X.
Shaw, Tucker, ***Confessions of a Backup Dancer.*** Simon & Schuster, 2004, 265pp. $8.99. ISBN: 0689870752.
Sorrells, Walter, ***Club Dread.*** Penguin, 2006, 272pp. $10.99. ISBN: 0525476180.
Triana, Gaby, ***Backstage Pass.*** HarperCollins, 2004, 224pp. $16.89. ISBN: 0060560177. HarperTrophy, 2005, 256pp. $7.99. ISBN: 0060560193.

Constable, Kate, *The Singer of All Songs.*

Chanters of Tremaris Trilogy. Scholastic, 2004, 297pp. $16.95. ISBN: 0439554780. Scholastic, 2005, 320pp. $4.99. ISBN: 0439554799. Random House Audio, 2004, $25. ISBN: 1400085144.

Web Site: <www.kateconstable.com>
Subjects: Disabilities, Friendship, Journeys, Magic, Music, Occupations, Prejudices, Relationships, Sailing, Self-Esteem, Wizards
Genres: Adventure, Fantasy
Levels: BL 7-10, K 7 up, PW 7 up, SLJ 6 up, V 7-12

Annotation: Sixteen-year-old Calwyn, a novice priestess of ice magic, helps Darrow, a wind chanter, escape under the frozen wall of Antaris and they join a group of chanters with different skills to stop a sorcerer who wants all of their powers for himself.

Booktalk: All morning long Calwyn walked along the Wall, singing without cease, checking for weaknesses or flaws. She was giddy with the magic that flowed from and around her. When Calwyn saw the man she thought she must be dreaming and her voice stopped for the first time since dawn. He was an Outlander with light colored hair and a face so pale it looked the color of ice. He shouldn't be here. He *couldn't* be here. There was no break in the Wall, no gap, no crack. She knew there wasn't. His being on this side of the Wall was not possible. Calwyn moved closer and bent down to look at him when suddenly his eyes popped open. Calwyn screamed and the stranger tried to pull himself up and began to sing a chant of Power. This was not good. She was forbidden to use her voice except in a Strengthening chant until the day's ritual was complete, but she had no choice. She sang up a spell of ice and cold but his spell of Power fought hers and when an unseen hand grabbed her from behind, Calwyn fell to the ground. She sat up dazed just as his strength gave out and he collapsed onto the path. What was Calwyn going to do with him now? Outlanders, especially men, were not allowed here. How was she going to explain how he got past the Wall? This didn't look good for a novice ice priestess.

Excerpt: Page 49 to break on page 53.

Curriculum Connections: Geography, History
Calwyn is surprised when Darrow carves a map of the world into an apple. Schedule time in the library media center for students to research early theories as to how the world is shaped, as well as determine why people were so upset by the idea that it is round.

Similar Titles:
Constable, Kate, ***The Tenth Power.*** Chanters of Tremaris Trilogy. Scholastic, 2006, 320pp. $16.99. ISBN: 0439554829. Random House Audio, 2006, $50. CD. ISBN: 1400090296.
Constable, Kate, ***The Waterless Sea.*** Chanters of Tremaris Trilogy. Scholastic, 2005, 320pp. $16.95. ISBN: 0439554802. Scholastic, 2006, 314pp. $5.99. ISBN: 0439554810. Listening Library, 2005, $30. ISBN: 1400090261.
Le Guin, Ursula, ***The Tombs of Atuan.*** The Earthsea Cycle. Simon & Schuster, 1991, 176pp. $21.95. ISBN: 0689316844. Simon & Schuster, 2001, 192pp. $6.99. ISBN: 0689845367.
Pierce, Tamora, ***Trickster's Choice.*** Daughter of the Lioness Series. Random House, 2003, 432pp. $17.95. ISBN: 0375814663. Random House, 2004, 448pp. $8.95. ISBN: 0375828796. Listening Library, 2003, $50.95. ISBN: 0807217913.
Pullman, Philip, ***The Golden Compass.*** His Dark Materials Series. Knopf, 1996, 399pp. $20. ISBN: 0679879242. Bantam Doubleday Dell, 2001, 399pp. $6.50. ISBN: 0440418321. Random House Audio, 1999, $37. ISBN: 0807281808.

24 Corrigan, Eireann, *Splintering.*

Scholastic, 2004, 184pp. $16.95. ISBN: 0439535972. Scholastic, 2004, 160pp. $7.99. ISBN: 043948992X.

Subjects: Brothers and Sisters, Crime, Depression, Drug Abuse, Emotional Problems, Sisters, Stress, Violence
Genres: Poetry, Realistic, Suspense
Lists: 2005 BBYA
Levels: BL 10-12, KL 9-12, PW 7 up, SLJ 9 up

Annotation: Poems, in alternating voices of 15-year-old Paulie and her older brother Jeremy, address their family's reaction during and after a PCP-crazed violent intruder attack while at their married sister's home.

Booktalk: Have you ever thought about how you were more scared after something terrible happened, than during it? Afterward is when you have time to think about how badly you could have been hurt for diving into the middle of a situation, even if you really had no choice. This terrible situation started because Paulie's older sister was having a rough time in her marriage and asked for company. Dad, mom, brother, and both sisters, the whole family, were at her house when it happened. They were all together in the same room when the PCP-crazed maniac with a machete broke into the house. At least they were *all* together for at least a few moments after the terror began. But Jeremy couldn't handle what was happening and ran and hid in the basement rather than staying upstairs to help his father protect his sisters and mother from a huge drug-crazed guy brandishing a machete. Their father tries to protect them, but his heart gives out and he falls to the floor. It is then up to Paulie, the younger sister, to become the heroine. Half of the book is told from Jeremy's perspective, so you will see how he is, or I should say isn't, dealing with his response to the attack. The other perspective is Paulie's, who had nothing but a splintering wooden door between her and a PCP-crazed man with a machete when her father collapsed. Will their perspectives of what happened be the same?

Excerpt: Page 55 through page 59.

Curriculum Connections: Creative Writing, English

Corrigan wrote this novel as free verse poems from two perspectives. Schedule time in the library media center for students to locate other free verse novels and collections of free verse poetry. Based on their reading and exploring of other poets' free verse writing styles, have students choose a scene from the novel and write a free verse poem, from a different character's perspective.

Similar Titles:

Corrigan, Eireann. **You Remind Me of You.** Push, 2002, 128pp. $6.99. ISBN: 0439297710.

Hemphill, Stephanie. **Things Left Unsaid: A Novel in Poems.** Hyperion, 2005, 272pp. $16.99. ISBN: 0786818506.

Herrick, Steven. **The Simple Gift.** Simon & Schuster, 2004, 188pp. $6.99. ISBN: 0689868677.

Lewis, Edward. **Hostile Ground: Defusing and Restraining Violent Behavior and Physical Assaults.** Paladin, 2000, 152pp. $20. ISBN: 1581600542.

Marcovitz, Hal. **PCP.** Thomson Gale, 2005, 112pp. $28.70. ISBN: 1590184203.

25 Coy, John, **Crackback**.
Scholastic, 2005, 208pp. $16.99. ISBN: 0439697336.

Web Site: <www.johncoy.com>
Subjects: Drug Abuse, Family Problems, Fathers and Sons, Football, Friendship, High Schools, Peer Pressure, Self-Esteem, Stress
Genres: Realistic, Sports
Lists: 2006 QP
Levels: BL 8-11, KL 6-12, SLJ 7 up

Annotation: Sophomore football player Miles is concerned about his best friend and other players taking steroids and the new win-at-all-costs coach, even though his ex-football playing father likes this new more aggressive style of play.

Booktalk: Miles is a football player who loves the game but not enough to buy into what the overzealous new coach is dishing. Miles is smart enough to see beyond the narrow sighted world the coach and some of the players live in, including his best friend Zach. When Miles refuses to take steroids along with Zach and the other players, he finds himself pretty much alone in the locker room. Life isn't any easier at home as his father was once a college football player and praising Miles for anything he does on the field, even a great play, just isn't within his capabilities. When Miles has to run laps for thinking on his own and running a play that the coach didn't call, his father knows about it before he even gets home from school and Miles hears about how stupid he is, loud and clear. There is no relief from his father's disapproval and verbal abuse. His mother and little sister try to avoid his anger by lowering their eyes and becoming mute, but Miles is a constant target. A target both at home and in the locker room. It isn't until a class assignment has Miles asking his uncle questions about his family that he learns the secret they have been hiding for years. It is the secret that has made his father an angry man. Miles must now decide what he will do with the information.

Excerpt: Page 1 to break on page 7.

Curriculum Connections: Biology, Health, Science
Schedule time in the library media center for students to research the use of steroids by football players and other sports stars. As a group, have them make a list of the various side effects that can occur when using steroids in improving performance.

Similar Titles:
Bissinger, H.G., **Friday Night Lights: A Town, a Team, and a Dream.** DeCapo Press, 2003, 384pp. $24. ISBN: 0306812827. Perseus Books Group, 2006, 357pp. $7.99. ISBN: 030681529X.
Cochran, Thomas, **Roughnecks.** Harcourt, 1999, 256pp. $6. ISBN: 0152022007.

Powell, Randy, ***Three Clams and an Oyster.*** Farrar, Straus & Giroux, 2002, 224pp. $16. ISBN: 0374375267. Farrar, Straus & Giroux, 2006, 224pp. $6.95. ISBN: 0374400075.

Spring, Albert, ***Steroids and Your Muscles: The Incredible Disgusting Story.*** Rosen, 2001, 48pp. $25.25. ISBN: 0823933938.

Tharp, Tim, ***Knights of the Hill Country.*** Knopf, 2006, 240pp. $16.95. ISBN: 0375836535.

Crutcher, Chris, **Whale Talk.**

Greenwillow, 2001, 224pp. $16.99. ISBN: 0688180191. Random House, 2002, 224pp. $6.99. ISBN: 0440229383. Listening Library, 2004, $32. ISBN: 0807207098. Listening Library, 2004, $45. CD. ISBN: 0807217786.

Web Site: <www.chriscrutcher.com>
Subjects: Adoption, African Americans, Bullying, Child Abuse, Disabilities, Emotional Problems, Fathers and Sons, Foster Homes, High Schools, Learning Disabilities, Peer Pressure, Physically Handicapped, Prejudices, Race Relations, Self-Esteem, Swimming, Teachers, Violence
Genres: Multicultural, Realistic, Sports
Lists: 2002 BBYA, 2003 SA, 2005 PP, 2005 B of BBYA
Levels: BL 8-12, PW 6 up, SLJ 8 up, V 10-12

Annotation: Athletically gifted multiracial TJ opts out of the regular school sports, but becomes captain of a swim team of misfits, evoking the ire of the jocks in school and the stepfather of the little African-American girl his parents take in as a foster child.

Booktalk: I was one of those little kids who acted out their frustrations through angry outbursts. When my mom and dad first adopted me they had a heck of a time dealing with my behavior and destructive actions, but they kept on loving me anyway. I know I am more fortunate than most kids whose biological mothers are drug addicts. Since those early days I have learned how to control my temper, but it isn't always easy. Especially when it comes to jerks like Mike Barbour. He and the other jocks think I sold out the school because I won't play on any of the sports teams. I try to ignore Barbour and his pals, but I had enough the day I came across him taunting brain damaged Chris Coughlin in the hallway and threatening Chris about what he would do to him if he wore his brother's football letterman jacket again. I told Barbour what I thought of him and tried to explain to Chris that it was okay for him to wear his dead brother's jacket, but Chris was too scared to understand and threw it in the trash. I took it out of the trash and gave it to him but Chris never wore it again. So, when Mr. Simet asked me to put together a swim team for him to coach I decided I knew who my first team mate would be—Chris Coughlin. If I thought Barbour was on my case before, it was nothing compared to what was to come when he and his friends realize the swim team could earn their own jackets.

Excerpt: First full paragraph on page 5 through break on page 8.

Curriculum Connections: Health, Physical Education, Psychology, Science
Each member of the swim team has a handicap to overcome as they meld themselves into a team. Schedule time in the library media center for students to research athletes with handicaps and share with the class how their chosen athlete overcame the limitations to compete in sports.

Similar Titles:
Crutcher, Chris, ***Ironman.*** Greenwillow, 1995, 192pp. $16.99. ISBN: 068813503X. HarperCollins, 2004, 279pp. $6.99. ISBN: 0060598409.
Crutcher, Chris, ***Stotan.*** Greenwillow, 1986, 192pp. $17.99. ISBN: 0688057152. HarperCollins, 2003, 272pp. $6.99. ISBN: 0060094923.
Forde, Catherine, ***Fat Boy Swim.*** Random House, 2004, 240pp. $15.95. ISBN: 0385732058. Random House, 2005, 240pp. $6.99. ISBN: 0440238919. Listening Library, 2004, $26. ISBN: 1400090415.
Laughlin, Terry, ***Total Immersion: A Revolutionary Way to Swim Better and Faster.*** Simon & Schuster, 2004, 302pp. $16. ISBN: 0743253434.
Oates, Joyce Carol, ***Sexy.*** HarperCollins, 2005. $17.89. ISBN: 0060541504. HarperCollins, 2006, 263pp. $7.99. ISBN: 0060541512.

27 Dines, Carol, *The Queen's Soprano.*
Harcourt, 2006, 336pp. $17. ISBN: 0152054774.

Subjects: Censorship, Cities, Family Problems, Fathers and Daughters, Mothers and Daughters, Music, Occupations, Opera, Relationships, Religion, Royalty, Runaways, Sexual Assault
Genres: Historical, International, Religious, Romance, Suspense
Lists: 2006 BBYA
Levels: BL 9-12, SLJ 9 up, V 5-12

Annotation: Seventeen-year-old Angelica Voglia, a gifted soprano, lives in Rome during the 1600s when Pope Innocent XI has banned women from singing in public. When her benefactor, a priest, and her biological father dies, Angelica runs away to the court of Queen Christina, who defies the Pope by allowing women to sing, before her mother can marry her off to the man who offers the most money.

Booktalk: I had not thought about why Father Zachary often came to our home when Father was away, or why he bought the mirror for me to sing in front of, or why he brought any of the other gifts that were only for me. I was both selfish and naïve. It wasn't until Lucia asked me why Father Zachary would take such personal care to help find my mother a husband that I began to wonder why he was so interested in me. But, it wasn't until she mentioned that I was born shortly after their marriage that I realize my beloved Papa is not my real father. I had just come to terms with this knowledge when Father Zachary dies and Mama decides to sell me off to the richest suitor. I am a Soprano and I have a voice that can make men cry. But few men have ever seen me as the Pope has decreed that women cannot sing in public. They hear me when I sing through an open upstairs window where they might catch a passing glimpse of me. The Pope thinks women's singing can inflame men to actions that are not within their control. I have heard that Queen Christina is defying the Pope's orders. She left Sweden and has a palace here in Rome where women are allowed to sing to audiences of both men and women. Do I allow Mama to sell me off to the highest bidder or do I run away to Queen Christina's Court? I have to make my decision soon as Mama is becoming more insane with greed every day.

Excerpt: Sixth paragraph on page 16 through page 21.

Curriculum Connections: History, Music
This novel is based on the life of the real Soprano, Angelica Voglia. Schedule time in the library media center for students to research Voglia as well as the Pope's law against women singing in public in late 17th century Rome.

Similar Titles:
Buckley, Veronica, ***Christina, Queen of Sweden: The Restless Life of a European Eccentric.*** HarperCollins, 2005, 385pp. $14.95. ISBN: 0060736186.
Dickinson, Peter, ***The Tears of the Salamander.*** Random House, 2003, 197pp. $16.95. ISBN: 0385730985. Random House, 2005, 208pp. $7.95. ISBN: 0440238234.
Hoffman, Mary, ***Stravaganza: City of Masks.*** Bloomsbury, 2002, 256pp. $17.95. ISBN: 1582347913. Bloomsbury, 2004, 352pp. $7.95. ISBN: 1582349177.
Hooper, Mary, ***The Remarkable Life and Times of Eliza Rose.*** Bloomsbury, 2006, 336pp. $16.95. ISBN: 1582348545.
Sturtevant, Katherine, ***A True and Faithful Narrative.*** Farrar, Straus & Giroux, 2006, 256pp. $17. ISBN: 0374378096.

Doyle, Malachy, *Georgie.*
Bloomsbury, 2002, 154pp. $13.95. ISBN: 1582347530. Bloomsbury, 2004, 156pp. $6.95. ISBN: 1582348995.

28

Web Site: <www.malachydoyle.co.uk>
Subjects: Boarding Schools, Death, Grieving, Mental Illness, Mothers and Sons, Murder, Orphans, Teachers, Violence
Genres: International, Realistic
Levels: BL 6-10, PW 7 up, SLJ 7-10

Annotation: Fourteen-year-old Georgie acts out in such a violent manner that no one has been able to reach him since as a very young child he saw his mother murdered. It takes Shannon, another disturbed teen, and a kind and patient teacher to bring Georgie out of his shell. Alternating chapters from Georgie and Shannon's perspectives.

Booktalk: I knew something was up when Ruby came into my room with my breakfast. They aren't supposed to do that. It isn't safe. I'm not nice in the morning. She eases herself into my room with the tray in front of her. She is trying to protect herself. Her eyes have a pleading look in them as she tells me that I am going to a new home in Wales. I just stare at her and don't even blink. This makes her even more nervous and she talks really fast. She is telling me about how I will have my own room and new friends. I can make a fresh start. A chance to begin again. And then she says it. "You'll have a chance to be normal." Normal? What does that mean? Ruby sees the look in my eyes and she knows she has gone too far. I pick up my cup of tea as if to drink it but I am holding it so hard the plastic handle digs into my hand. I can't control my anger anymore and I throw the cup and the tea runs down the door, adding another stain to the many already there. I am not leaving here. This is all I deserve. A mattress on a bare floor. I know this is all I deserve.

Excerpt: From break on page 20 to break on page 24.

Curriculum Connections: Creative Writing, English, Psychology
Georgie is written in alternating first person perspectives. Schedule time in the library media center for students to research child and teen responses to violence in their lives. Based on what they have learned about the various ways others have dealt with, or not dealt with, the aftermath of family violence, have students choose one of the scenes in the novel and rewrite it with themselves present and how they would interact with Georgie.

Similar Titles:
Connelly, Neil, **St. Michael's Scales.** Scholastic, 2002, 320pp. $16.95. ISBN: 0439194458. Scholastic, 2004, 320pp. $6.99. ISBN: 0439491711.
Halliday, John, **Shooting Monarchs.** Simon & Schuster, 2003, 144pp. $15.95. ISBN: 0689843380.
I Wrote on All Four Walls: Teens Speak Out on Violence. Annick Press, 2004, 144pp. $19.95. ISBN: 1550377574. Annick Press, 2004, 144pp. $9.95. ISBN: 1550377566.
McCormick, Patricia, **Cut.** Front Street, 2000, 168pp. $16.95. ISBN: 1886910618. Scholastic, 2002, 160pp. $6.95. ISBN: 0439324599.
Zephaniah, Benjamin, **Gangsta Rap.** Bloomsbury, 2004, 200pp. $7.95. ISBN: 1582348863.

Draper, Sharon M., *Copper Sun.*
Atheneum, 2006, 306pp. $16.95. ISBN: 0689821816.

Web Site: <SharonDraper.com>
Subjects: Africans, African Americans, Friendship, Journeys, Prejudices, Race Relations, Rape, Runaways, Slavery
Genres: Historical, Multicultural
Levels: BL 9-12, PW 9 up, SLJ 8 up

Annotation: Fifteen-year-old Amari is kidnapped from her African village, sold into slavery, and bought by a cruel plantation owner in the Carolinas. The indentured white girl Polly and Amari become friends and escape together to Fort Mose.

Booktalk: Amari was the spoiled daughter who often snuck off into the jungle instead of helping her mother and the other village women with the cooking and spinning. She knew she was to marry the tall good looking Besa the next year when she turned sixteen. Even the sound of his voice made her tremble in anticipation of being his wife. The day the world turned upside down for Amari was the day Besa came to the village to tell the elders that there was a group of men with pale faces coming down the path. The village hurried to welcome them with a celebration of food, drink, and dancing. The repayment for their welcome was the slaughter of the elders and young and the enslavement of the men and women. Many never made it through the jungle and into the slave prison. And many of those that did died in the hold of the ship and were fed to the sharks. Amari did not die, but she felt dead inside. Afi, the older woman who was chained to her, kept telling Amari that she had to live. She could not give up because she must show them that she was a proud daughter of Africa. Amari made it through the Middle Passage to America, only to be sold to a sadist plantation owner as a birthday gift for his 16-year-old son. Amari had to figure out a way out of this degradation.

Excerpt: Page 25 through page 27.

Curriculum Connections: History
Amari and Polly do not travel North as most runaway slaves did, but went South to Fort Mose. Schedule time in the library media center for students to research this Spanish fort that welcomed runaway slaves.

Similar Titles:
Deagan, Kathleen A., *Fort Mose: Colonial America's Black Fortress of Freedom.* University Press of Florida, 1995, 53pp. $16.95. ISBN: 0813013526.
Growing Up in Slavery: Stories of Young Slaves as Told by Themselves. Lawrence Hill Books, 2005, 256pp. $22.95. ISBN: 1556525486. Lawrence Hill Books, 2007, 256pp. $9.95. ISBN: 1556526350.
Jacobs, Harriet, *Incidents in the Life of a Slave Girl.* Signet Classic, 2000, 256pp. $5.95. ISBN: 0451527526.

McCafferty, Kate, ***Testimony of an Irish Slave Girl.*** Viking, 2002, 224pp. $24.95. ISBN: 0670030651. Penguin, 2003, 224pp. $13. ISBN: 014200183X.
Rinaldi, Ann, ***Hang a Thousand Trees with Ribbons.*** Harcourt, 2005, 352pp. $6.95. ISBN: 015205393X.

30 Fiedler, Lisa, *Romeo's Ex: Rosaline's Story.*
Holt, 2006, 246pp. $16.95. ISBN: 0805075003.

Subjects: Cities, Death, Family Problems, Fathers and Daughters, Friendship, Jealousy, Medicine, Murder, Relationships, Royalty, Sexual Relationships, Suicide, Violence
Genres: Historical, International, Romance
Levels: K 6-12, KL 6-12, PW 6 up, SLJ 7 up

Annotation: Rosaline, the 16-year-old cousin of Juliette Capulet, has spurned Romeo Montague's declarations of love but she becomes romantically involved with another Montague, adding to the intrigue. The story is told from multiple perspectives within the feuding families.

Booktalk: Have you ever been in a situation where you and several other people witnessed or were involved in the same event and later realized your versions of what had occurred were quite different? Personal perspective has quite a way of shaping how you relate the incidents, doesn't it? For example, would your description of someone be different if you found his or her romantic attentions toward you irritating rather than flattering? That is certainly the case for Rosaline, who is not the least bit interested in the romantic attentions of Romeo. Yes, Shakespeare's Romeo, but Rosaline isn't about to be pining for the handsome young Montague. No "Romeo, Romeo, where art thou Romeo!" laments from this young woman. Rosaline would more likely be saying, "Get thee out, Romeo!" If you don't already know the whole tale, Romeo had initially fallen head over heels in love with Rosaline, Juliette's older cousin, and was following her around like a love sick puppy. But Rosaline knew Romeo was nothing but a handsome young fop whose eye would soon roam to someone else. And the someone else was her little cousin Juliette. Naïve Juliette fell for Romeo's sweet words and before anyone in either of their families or groups of friends knew about them, their relationship tore apart what little calm there was in Verona between the Capulets and the Montagues. Rosaline, and the Montague "enemy" she has fallen in love with, are also caught up in the intrigue. There are more secret meetings going on in Verona than those of Romeo and Juliette.

Excerpt: From break on page 12 through page 16.

Curriculum Connections: Creative Writing, Drama, English
Rosaline is a character in Shakespeare's well known play who is often not remembered, but who has her own perspective of the situation between the feuding

families. Schedule time in the library media center for students to research the various secondary characters in the play. After researching their chosen character, ask students to write the dialogue they think may have happened between their character and Rosaline.

Similar Titles:

Draper, Sharon M., ***Romiette and Julio.*** Atheneum, 1999, 240pp. $17.95. ISBN: 0689821808. Simon Pulse, 2001, 336pp. $6.99. ISBN: 0689842090.

Fiedler, Lisa, ***Dating Hamlet: Ophelia's Story.*** Holt, 2002, 176pp. $16.95. ISBN: 0805070540.

Klein, Lisa, ***Ophelia.*** Bloomsbury, 2006, 336pp. $16.95. ISBN: 1582348014.

Manga Shakespeare: Romeo and Juliet. Manga Shakespeare. Abrams, 2007, 208pp. $9.95. ISBN: 0810993252.

Meyer, Carolyn, ***Loving Will Shakespeare.*** Harcourt, 2006, 272pp. $17. ISBN: 0152054510.

Flinn, Alex, *Diva.*

HarperCollins, 2006, 263pp. $17.89. ISBN: 0060568453.

Web Site: <www.alexflinn.com>
Subjects: Body Image, High Schools, Mothers and Daughters, Music, Opera, Peer Pressure, Self-Esteem, Teachers, Weight Control
Genres: Realistic
Levels: KL 10-12, SLJ 7-10

Annotation: Sixteen-year-old Caitlin leaves behind her old high school and a previous abusive boyfriend to attend Miami High School of the Arts, where even as a musician she does not easily fit in due to her dream of becoming an opera singer.

Booktalk: I'm Caitlin, but you can call me Opera Grrrl, with three "r"s and no "i". That's what I call myself in my online journal. I love my blog. That's where I can be myself. Some people think I am a bit weird because I love opera. My dream is to someday be on stage as a real diva, like Maria Callas. I know that teenage girls and opera don't normally go together but for me it works. When I sing, I forget about everything else. Even though opera is a performing art, I sometimes feel out of place at the Miami High School of the Arts where I was recently accepted. But I am developing a few friendships. I haven't gotten up the courage to join Gus's conga line yet, but I did join in with Peyton and Ashley when Gigi started singing "All That Jazz" from *Chicago* at the train station. Okay, so it took me a few lines into it, but I joined in and it felt good. It was the first time I felt like maybe I could belong in this school. No one knows about my last school and what happened with Nick and I want it to stay that way. I still have some self-esteem problems after the way he treated me. And I still don't get along with my mom, who wants to be friends instead of a parent, but I am working on being me—Caitlin, a girl who knows she worries about her weight too much, but who also knows she can sing opera.

Excerpt: Page 30 to first break on page 35.

Curriculum Connections: History, Music
Schedule time in the library media center for students to research the history of one of the operas that Caitlin discusses in her online journal. Ask students to relate the events in the opera to events that are occurring in the world today.

Similar Titles:
Conway, Celeste, *The Melting Season.* Random House, 2006, 288pp. $17.99. ISBN: 038590357X.
Flinn, Alex, *Breathing Underwater.* HarperCollins, 2001, 272pp. $17.99. ISBN: 0060291982. HarperTeen, 2002, 272pp. $7.99. ISBN: 0064472574.
L'Engle, Madeleine, *Small Rain.* Farrar, Straus & Giroux, 1985, 271pp. $15. ISBN: 0374519129.
Nolan, Han, *Born Blue.* Harcourt, 2001, 288pp. $17. ISBN: 0152019162. Harcourt, 2003, 300pp. $6.95. ISBN: 0152046976.
Simon, H.W., *100 Great Operas and Their Stories.* Knopf, 1989, 560pp. $16. ISBN: 0385054483.

32 Flinn, Alex, *Fade to Black.*

HarperCollins, 2005, 184pp. $17.89. ISBN: 006058410. HarperCollins, 2006, 208pp. $6.99. ISBN: 0060568429.

Web Site: <www.alexflinn.com>
Subjects: Brothers and Sisters, Bullying, Disabilities, Divorce, Fathers and Sons, High Schools, Hispanics, HIV/AIDS, Learning Disabilities, Moving, Peer Pressure, Prejudices, Race Relations, Violence
Genres: Multicultural, Realistic
Levels: BL 7-10, KL 6-12, SLJ 8 up

Annotation: Seventeen-year-old HIV positive Alex Crusan is attacked in a small Florida town and everyone thinks it is fellow student Clinton Cole since he hasn't been shy about his dislike of Alex being in his classes or their younger sisters playing together.

Booktalk: I just don't get it. Why would they even let this guy enroll in school? Not only is he in our school but he is in my class, sitting near me. What if he coughs or breathes on me, or something? And to top it off my mom is letting my sister play with his little sister. Maybe I did let my anger get a little out of hand when Mom let Melody spend the night over there. After Melody got home I went a little crazy and rode over to Crusan's house and threw a rock through their window. I don't think Crusan knows I'm the one putting notes in his locker telling him to get out of Pinedale. But, that's all I have done. So, when the cops showed up to talk to me I didn't tell them a darn thing. After all, I really didn't do anything directly to him. Maybe I did say a few things to other people that make it clear that I think that Crusan should be sent packing back to Miami. They don't have anything on me. No one saw me throw that rock. Wait a minute! The cops are saying someone saw me leaving the scene of the crime. And the scene of the crime is Crusan's busted up red SUV, where supposedly I beat him up with a baseball bat and now he's in the hospital. I may want him gone, but I don't want him *dead*. Honestly I don't. Who is this witness who says they saw me?

Excerpt: Last paragraph beginning on page 38 through page 43.

Curriculum Connections: Health
Schedule time in the library media center for students to research HIV/AIDS statistics for teenagers in the United States. Have students discuss these statistics and the personal narratives of HIV positive teens in relation to their background knowledge of HIV/AIDS prior to testing positive.

Similar Titles:
Flinn, Alex, ***Nothing to Lose.*** HarperCollins, 2004, 288pp. $15.95. ISBN: 0060517506. HarperTeen, 2005, 288pp. $6.99. ISBN: 0060517522.
Hyde, Margaret O., ***Safe Sex 101: An Overview for Teens.*** Twentieth Century Books, 2006, 128pp. $26.60. ISBN: 0822534398.
Kerr, M.E., ***Night Kites.*** HarperCollins, 1987, 256pp. $5.99. ISBN: 0064470350.
Minchin, Adele, ***The Beat Goes On.*** Simon & Schuster, 2004, 212pp. $16.95. ISBN: 0689866119.
Winick, Judd, ***Pedro and Me: Friendship, Loss and What I Learned.*** Holt, 2000, 192pp. $16. ISBN: 0805064036.

Frank, E.R., *America.*

Atheneum, 2002, 242pp. $18. ISBN: 0689847297. Simon & Schuster, 2003, 256pp. $7.99. ISBN: 0689857721.

33

Subjects: African Americans, Child Abuse, Child Sexual Abuse, Emotional Problems, Foster Homes, Journals, Mental Illness, Prejudices, Race Relations, Runaways, Suicide, Violence, Writing
Genres: Multicultural, Realistic
Lists: 2003 BBYA
Levels: BL 10-12, KL 9-12, PW 6 up, SLJ 8 up, V 10-12

Annotation: From ages 15 to 18, multiracial America describes, via his journal entries written while in Ridgeway Hospital, his life in foster homes, living on the street, surviving sexual abuse, and attempting suicide.

Booktalk: When I was little my adoptive family gave me away because I started to look my color. Mamma named me America because she didn't know who my father was. I guess I was supposed to belong to everyone, but I really belonged to no one. For a while I lived with Mrs. Harper after that family said they didn't want me because I was part black. Then I had to go back to my mother but she went out one night to get drugs and never came back. I lived on the streets and finally I got back to Mrs. Harper. She was old by then, but I was nine and I knew I could help her out. Browning, her stepbrother, was there too. He was supposed to be helping her too, but he spent most of his time with me. At first it was baseball and that was fun, but then he said he was going to teach me how to read. I got nervous when he said Mrs. Harper wasn't going to like how he was going to teach me so I had better keep it our secret. He held up the first flash card and it had an S on it. I knew how to pronoun that—ssss, like a snake. Then came the H flash card. I knew that one too. Both letters together make a shhh sound, like be quiet. But the next two letters I didn't want to sound out. I knew that adding those sounds made a bad word. Browning told me I had to say it so I did. I was so worried Mrs. Harper would hear and get mad at me. It just got worse. Pretty soon I was reading magazines out loud to Browning with words in them lots worst than the shhh word. That was a long time ago, but I still can't get those words and pictures out of my head.

Excerpt: Page 1 through page 2.

Curriculum Connections: English, History, Sociology
America said his mother gave him his name because it signified what he was—multiracial like the United States. Schedule time in the library media center for students to research the history and meaning of names, choosing a name they think fits America.

Similar Titles:
Anderson, Laurie Halse, ***Speak.*** Farrar, Straus & Giroux, 1999, 198pp. $16. ISBN: 0374371520. Penguin Putnam, 2001, 208pp. $7.99. ISBN: 014131088X. Bantam Books Audio, 2000, $22. ISBN: 0807282642.
Burgess, Melvin, ***Smack.*** Holt, 1998, 326pp. $16.95. ISBN: 080505801X. HarperTeen, 1999, 304pp. $6.99. ISBN: 0380732238.
Carter, William Lee, ***It Happened to Me: A Teen's Guide to Overcoming Sexual Abuse.*** New Harbinger, 2002, 180pp. $17.95. ISBN: 1572242795.
Chbosky, Stephen, ***The Perks of Being a Wallflower.*** MTV/Pocket, 1999, 213pp. $12. ISBN: 0671027344. Books on Tape, 2001, $24.95. ISBN: 0736649360.
Frank, E.R., ***Wrecked.*** Simon & Schuster, 2005, 247pp. $15.95. ISBN: 0689873832. Simon Pulse, 2007, 256pp. $8.99. ISBN: 0689873840.

Fredericks, Mariah, *Crunch Time.*

Atheneum, 2006, 317pp. $15.95. ISBN: 068986938X. Simon Pulse, 2007, 336pp. $7.99. ISBN: 1416939733.

Subjects: Fathers and Sons, Friendship, High Schools, Mothers and Daughters, Peer Pressure, Self-Esteem, Stress, Testing, Universities and Colleges
Genres: Realistic
Levels: BL 8-11, PW 6 up, SLJ 9 up

Annotation: Four juniors from a Manhattan private school, who would not be in each other's social groups, skip out of their SAT preparation classes to study together.

Booktalk: I remember taking my SATs and bombing the math section, but I don't remember stressing about it. But that certainly isn't the case with the four juniors in this book. Daisy is worried because she needs a high score to be eligible for financial aid. Jane basically doesn't care, but as the daughter of a movie star she is expected to care. Max is trying to get a higher score so that, for once, his father will not tell him he can do better. And Leo's the one who wants to be perfect, not that his father cares. These four unlikely "friends" gather at Jane's swanky NYC apartment to study for the SAT. But there is more going on than studying. Max is thinking about Daisy and how to get her to think of him as other than a friend. But Daisy is attracted to bad boys and Leo is going to be her next bad decision. Jane just wants someone to notice her (other than her stepfather) and like her for herself, not because she is her mother's daughter. Then, all heck breaks loose at school when an "A" student steps forward and admits she took the test for someone else, but won't say who. The rumors are really flying. Who is the cheater? One of the four?

Excerpt: Page 32 through page 37.

Curriculum Connections: Career Education
Schedule time in the library media center for students to research the use and validity of college entrance exams. Based on their research, have students discuss their view of the validity of these tests in relation to long-term success in college.

Similar Titles:
Cappo, Nan Willard, *Cheating Lessons.* Atheneum, 2002, 240pp. $16. ISBN: 068984378X. Simon Pulse, 2003, 272pp. $4.99. ISBN: 0689860188.
Fredericks, Mariah, *The True Meaning of Cleavage.* Atheneum, 2003, 224pp. $15.95. ISBN: 0689850921. Simon Pulse, 2004, 240pp. $6.99. ISBN: 0689869584.
Marcovitz, Hal, *Teens and Cheating.* Mason Crest, 2005, 112pp. $22.95. ISBN: 1590848713.
The New Rules of College Admissions: Ten Former Administration Officers

Reveal What It Takes to Get into College Today. Simon & Schuster, 2006, 272pp. $14. ISBN: 0743280679. Blackstone Audio, 2006, $65.95. ISBN: 0786147679. Blackstone Audio, 2006, $81. CD. ISBN: 0786163771.

Steele, Julia, *The Taker.* Hyperion, 2006, 240pp. $15.99. ISBN: 0786849304.

35 Gantos, Jack, *The Love Curse of the Rumbaughs.*

Farrar, Straus & Giroux, 2006, 185pp. $17. ISBN: 0374336903. Listening Library, 2006, $30. ISBN: 0739335685. Listening Library, 2006, $30. CD. ISBN: 0307286126.

Web Site: <www.jackgantos.com>
Subjects: Death, Elderly, Genetics, Grieving, Medical Experimentation, Mothers and Daughters, Mothers and Sons
Genres: Horror, Mystery
Levels: BL 10-12, PW 6 up, SLJ 8 up, V 7-12

Annotation: In a small Pennsylvania town, Ivy has inherited the curse of excess love for one's mother and does not consider the elderly twins' use of taxidermy to keep their mother's body with them unusual as she plans to do the same to her mother when she dies.

Booktalk: Families keep the strangest secrets. My mother, who was very young when she had me, told me that our family secret was my father's identity. I asked her who he is all the time but she just said that she would tell me when I turned 16. In the mean time I grew up in the pharmacy with Abner and Adolph Rumbaugh, who everyone calls the Twins. They have "always" owned this pharmacy. My mother started working there when she was a teenager. They are old, very old and move very slowly but they are as much a part of my life as my mother. Nothing exciting about them. I thought finding out who my father was would be the biggest news of my life, but I had no idea that his identity also meant I was cursed. I waited 16 years to find out I was cursed with the love curse of the Rumbaughs. It didn't take quite so long to understand what the curse meant and what it can do to you when it really kicks in. Even though my mother had tried to hide their weirdness from me, I already knew about the Twins and what they had done to their mother. I was long over that. I found her in the basement one day, "stuffed like a hibernating bear." It wasn't that seeing a stuffed old lady was all that scary. What was scary was my little girl's realization that the Twins had loved their mother as much as I love mine. Preserving their mother in whatever form they could to keep her with them didn't seem all that odd to me. I told my mother, "Don't worry. Someday I'll do that to you too." Instead of being happy, she was mortified and whispered, "Oh, my God, you have the curse!" She wouldn't tell me back then what the curse was, but now I know. I've been practicing my taxidermy skills on the dead animals I find. The Twins are helping me. I have plenty of time before my mother gets old. But, I can feel the love curse ticking away inside of me. Maybe it is so strong now because I know who my father is, well sort of.

Excerpt: Page 7 to break on page 12.

Curriculum Connections: Biology, Psychology, Science
The subjects of nature vs. nurture and eugenics are addressed in this novel. Schedule time in the library media center for student to research early scientific findings and positions on eugenics and discuss how research methods and findings have changed through the years.

Similar Titles:
Bradbury, Ray, ***Something Wicked This Way Comes.*** HarperCollins, 1999, 293pp. $15.95. ISBN: 0380977273. HarperCollins, 1998, 304pp. $6.99. ISBN: 0380729407.
Gantos, Jack, ***Hole In My Life.*** Farrar, Straus & Giroux, 2003, 200pp. $16. ISBN: 0374399883. Farrar, Straus & Giroux, 2003, 208pp. $8. ISBN: 0374430896.
Gothic!: Ten Original Dark Tales. Candlewick, 2004, 256pp. $15.99. ISBN: 0763622435. Candlewick, 2006, 256pp. $7.99. ISBN: 0763627372.
Kevles, Daniel, ***In the Name of Eugenics: Genetics and the Uses of Human Heredity.*** Harvard University Press, 1998, 448pp. $21.95. ISBN: 0674445570.
Werlin, Nancy, ***Double Helix.*** Dial, 2004, 252pp. $15.99. ISBN: 0803726066. Penguin, 2005, 256pp. $6.99. ISBN: 014240327X.

Garden, Nancy, ***Endgame.***
Harcourt, 2006, 287pp. $17. ISBN: 0152054162.

Web Site: <http://members.aol.com/nancygarden>
Subjects: Brothers, Bullying, Crime, Death, Emotional Problems, Fathers and Sons, High Schools, Mental Illness, Moving, Murder, Peer Pressure, Self-Esteem, Violence
Genres: Realistic
Levels: PW 9 up, SLJ 8 up, V 7-12

Annotation: Conversations between 15-year-old Gray Wilton, who is the target of the bullies at school, and his attorney while Gray is on trial for murder after taking his father's gun to school and shooting fellow students, tell a story of severe harassment and the result when the victim is pushed over the edge.

Booktalk: Gray was hoping things would change when they moved to Connecticut. His dad said it would be a new start and that records from middle school don't follow you to high school. So Gray was being offered a clean slate. There would be no references to the two suspensions from middle school. Things were okay during the summer but as soon as school started Gray realized that nothing had changed. The bullies were just older and meaner. Zorro, the captain of the football team, almost immediately zeroed in on him as his new target to torment and began bouncing Gray off lockers and calling him Crater Face. Having his new friend Ross to hang out with and join him in vicariously killing Zorro and his buddies in video games made the abuse at school a bit easier to take, but Gray absolutely hated going to school. His parents knew something was wrong and reacted as they always did. His dad got mad and told him to be a man while his mom made excuses for him. The attacks escalated as the year went on and when Gray's drum set, brought to school for the Christmas concert against his father's wishes, was trashed in the music room, Gray knew it was Zorro and said so. Bad idea. Zorro and his sidekick ambushed Gray near the art room and forced him to drink black paint. Upchucking in the art room trash can and a trip to the nurse, who Gray told exactly what had happened and who did it to him, didn't stop the harassment. The teachers and the principal ignored the "horseplay" of their star athlete and his buddies. But it was the next attack, in the locker room where no one could see what they forced Gray and Ross to do, that pushes Gray over the edge. Gray's life, and the lives of many others, would never be the same again, at least for those who survived.

Excerpt: From break on page 9 to break on page 15.

Curriculum Connections: Psychology
Have students reread the Epilogue before scheduling time in the library media center to research school shootings and court verdicts. Based on what they learned about real life situations, have students discuss whether or not they think Gray's sentence was appropriate.

Similar Titles:
Koja, Kathe, ***Buddha Boy.*** Farrar, Straus & Giroux, 2003, 128pp. $16. ISBN: 0374309981. Penguin, 2004, 128pp. $5.99. ISBN: 0142402095.
Myers, Walter Dean, ***Shooter.*** HarperCollins, 2004, 224pp. $16.89. ISBN: 0060295201. HarperCollins, 2005, 223pp. $6.99. ISBN: 0064472906. HarperAudio, 2004, $22. ISBN: 006074765X.
Olin, Sean, ***Killing Britney.*** Simon Pulse, 2005, 234pp. $8.99. ISBN: 0689877781.
Prose, Francine, ***After.*** HarperCollins, 2003, 306pp. $16.99. ISBN: 0060080817. HarperCollins, 2004, 336pp. $7.99. ISBN: 0060080833.
Strasser, Todd, ***Give a Boy a Gun.*** Simon & Schuster, 2002, 208pp. $5.99. ISBN: 0689848935.

37 Geras, Adele, *Ithaka.*

Harcourt, 2006, 368pp. $17. ISBN: 0152056033. Harcourt, 2007, 368pp. $6.95. ISBN: 0152061045.
Web Site: <www.adelegeras.com>
Subjects: Gods and Goddesses, Jealousy, Journeys, Relationships, Sailing, Self-Esteem, War
Genres: Fantasy, Historical, International, Romance
Lists: 2006 BBYA
Levels: BL 10-12, PW 9 up, SLJ 9 up, V 10-12

Annotation: Pining for the love of Telemachus, 14-year-old Klymene, who is able to see and speak to the gods and goddesses, is the faithful servant to Queen Penelope as her mistress deals with ardent suitors while weaving and waiting for Odysseus to return.

Booktalk: I was transported back to Ithaka and felt the rocks under my sandals as I walked the paths of this ancient island with young Klymene as she agonized over her love for Odysseus and Penelope's son Telemachus. Woe is Klymene. He has fallen under the seductive spell of the selfish but beautiful Melantho. Doesn't it seem like there is always someone who gets in the way when you are trying to connect with your one true love? Clearly, from Klymene's agony over Telemachus' infatuation with the very forward Melantho and his callous treatment of the one who truly loves him, relationships weren't much different back in Ancient Greece. But it isn't just Klymene who is having relationship problems. Penelope is patiently waiting for her beloved Odysseus to return as she weaves the story of his return on her loom. She waits, even though his husband's own father does not believe his son is alive and wishes her to remarry. Her weaving days may be over when Leodes, a childhood friend of Odysseus, arrives on the island as a suitor and Penelope falls under the spell of love. Enter a tale of love and deceit, where gods and goddesses interfere in the lives of mortals.

Excerpt: From the break on page 73 through page 75.

Curriculum Connections: Creative Writing, Drama, English, History
Schedule time in the library media center for students to research the various Greek gods and goddesses Geras includes in this novel. After choosing a god or goddess, have students write the dialogue they would have with their chosen deity in relation to helping Klymene or Penelope out of the situation in which they find themselves.

Similar Titles:
Cooney, Caroline B., ***Goddess of Yesterday.*** Delacorte, 2002, 264pp. $15.95. ISBN: 0385729456. Laurel Leaf, 2002, 272pp. $6.50. ISBN: 0440229308.
Geras, Adele, ***Troy.*** Harcourt, 2002, 376pp. $6.95. ISBN: 0152045708.
McLaren, Clemence, ***Inside the Walls of Troy.*** Simon & Schuster, 2004, 208pp. $5.99. ISBN: 0689873972.
McLaren, Clemence, ***Waiting for Odysseus.*** Simon Pulse, 2004, 160pp. $5.99. ISBN: 0689867050.
Sutcliff, Rosemary, ***Black Ships Before Troy: The Story of the Iliad.*** Laurel Leaf, 2005, 160pp. $5.99. ISBN: 055349483X.

38 Giles, Gail, *Dead Girls Don't Write Letters.*
Roaring Brook, 2003, 156pp. $15.95. ISBN: 0761317279. Simon Pulse, 2004, 128pp. $6.99. ISBN: 0689866240.

Web Site: <www.gailgiles.com>
Subjects: Alcoholism, Death, Depression, Emotional Problems, Family Problems, Fires, Grieving, Jealousy, Letter Writing, Mental Illness, Mothers and Daughters, Self-Esteem, Sisters
Genres: Mystery, Realistic, Suspense
Lists: 2004 QP
Levels: BL 6-9, PW 6 up, SLJ 9 up

Annotation: Ninth-grader Sunny is dealing with her parents' grief over her 18-year-old sister's death in an apartment fire until an imposter arrives, insisting she is Jazz and that the badly burned body was not hers.

Booktalk: Sunny was not the least bit upset when she heard that her older sister Jazz died in a fire. She was glad to be rid of Jazz and her manipulative behavior, but no such luck. Jazz just won't go away! First the bright yellow envelope shows up in the mailbox. Sunny had gone home at lunch time to try to get her mother to eat something when she found the letter in the mailbox. Even though Sunny was sure it was Jazz's handwriting, the letter could wait until she got back home from school later that afternoon. No point in getting upset about it now. It can wait. Besides, dead girls can't write letters, can they? Later that afternoon Sunny discovers that apparently they can. The letter says Jazz wasn't in the apartment when the building caught fire and she just found out that her family thinks she's dead. While they suffered, she had been away acting in a play. Jazz will be home in a few days. Sunny's deeply depressed mother is out of her bathrobe and making brownies for her beloved Jazz. Her father has put the bottle down, at least for a little while, to welcome his favorite daughter home. But when the tall willowy girl arrives at their front door Sunny knows that this girl isn't Jazz. But who is she and how does she know the smallest details of their lives?

Excerpt: Page 7 through page 10.

Curriculum Connections: Biology, Health, Science
Schedule time in the library media center for students to research the latest techniques in forensic science. These advances help ensure that errors in body identification do not occur as frequently as they have in the past.

Similar Titles:
Koja, Kathe, *Going Under.* Farrar, Straus & Giroux, 2006, 128pp. $16. ISBN: 0374303932.
Oates, Joyce Carol, *After the Wreck, I Picked Myself Up, Spread My Wings, and Flew Away.* HarperCollins, 2006, 304pp. $16.99. ISBN: 0060735252.

Picoult, Jodi, ***My Sister's Keeper.*** Simon & Schuster, 2004, 423pp. $25. ISBN: 0743454529. Simon & Schuster, 2005, 423pp. $14. ISBN: 0743454537. Recorded Books, 2004, $34.99. ISBN: 1402573219. Recorded Books, 2005, $29.99. CD. ISBN: 1419364375.

Schutz, Samantha, ***I Don't Want to Be Crazy.*** Scholastic Push, 2006, 288pp. $16.99. ISBN: 043980518X.

Wittlinger, Ellen, ***The Long Night of Leo and Bree.*** Simon & Schuster, 2002, 128pp. $15. ISBN: 0689835647. Simon Pulse, 2003, 128pp. $6.99. ISBN: 0689863357.

39

Giles, Gail, ***Playing in Traffic.***

Roaring Brook, 2004, 176pp. ISBN: 1596430052. Simon Pulse, 2006, 176pp. $6.99. ISBN: 1416909265.

Web Site: <www.gailgiles.com>
Subjects: Brothers and Sisters, Emotional Problems, Family Problems, High Schools, Mental Illness, Peer Pressure, Relationships, Self-Esteem, Sexual Relationships, Violence
Genres: Realistic, Suspense
Lists: 2003 BBYA, 2005 QP, 2005 B of BBYA
Levels: BL 8-12, PW 9 up, SLJ 10 up

Annotation: Goth girl Skye has set her sights on 17-year-old nerdy Matt and uses sex and lies about her family to try to manipulate him into an act of violence against them.

Booktalk: I have always been a fairly quiet kid but after the guy showed up at our house and we found out my dad had been seeing another woman, I got even quieter. That happened while I was in middle school. I'm in high school and not a whole lot more outgoing. I hang out with my friends Ken and Jeremy but we are not what you would call the popular guys in school. That is why I was so surprised when she purposely rammed into me. I was at my locker when she slammed up against my hip and then rolled around behind me so that her butt was up against mine before she was back in my face telling me that she was Skye. Like I didn't know who she was! Everyone in school knows Skye is the dark and deadly one. She is beautiful, but oh so deadly. And, way out of my league. I found my way to class but I wasn't focused on English, that's for sure. I was focused on the idea of her butt up against me. I returned to my locker after class and there was a piece of notebook paper sticking out of it. At first I thought the red was blood as I had heard Skye was a cutter, but it was just sticky red lipstick. It said "Park. 7. You know you want to." Well, of course I wanted to, but come on! It wasn't like I had the guts to go through with it. That's why I couldn't believe I was actually getting out of my car in the parking lot and walking over to her. There she was, with a smug look on her face. She knew I would show up. Then she whispered in my ear that she had picked me out. If I had only known then what she had picked me out to do.

Excerpt: Page 29 through page 30.

Curriculum Connections: Health, Psychology
Matt's younger sister Katy makes the statement that one of her friends considers anorexia a lifestyle choice rather than a disease. Schedule time in the library media center for students to locate first person narratives of teens who have suffered from anorexia and determine if they too thought of anorexia as a "lifestyle choice."

Similar Titles:
Bone, Ian, *Sleep Rough Tonight.* Dutton, 2005, 256pp. $16.99. ISBN: 0525473734.
Draper, Sharon M., *The Battle of Jericho.* Atheneum, 2003, 304pp. $17.95. ISBN: 0689842325. Simon Pulse, 2003, 352pp. $5.99. ISBN: 0689842333.
Giles, Gail, *Shattering Glass.* Roaring Brook, 2002, 224pp. $17.95. ISBN: 0761315810. Simon Pulse, 2003, 224pp. $6.99. ISBN: 0689858000.
Jenkins, A.M., *Out of Order.* HarperCollins, 2003, 256pp. $16.89. ISBN: 0066239699. HarperTeen, 2005, 256pp. $6.99. ISBN: 0064473740.
Klass, David, *Dark Angel.* Farrar, Straus & Giroux, 2005, 230pp. $17. ISBN: 0374399506. HarperTeen, 2007, 320pp. $7.99. ISBN: 0060887001.

40 Green, John, *Looking for Alaska.*

Dutton, 2005, 221pp. $15.99. ISBN: 0525475060. Penguin, 2006, 256pp. $7.99. ISBN: 0142402516. Brilliance Audio, 2006, $39.25. ISBN: 1423324471. Brilliance Audio, 2006, $82.25. CD. ISBN: 1423324455.

Web Site: <www.sparksflyup.com>
Subjects: Accidents, Alcohol Abuse, Boarding Schools, Body Image, Death, Emotional Problems, Friendship, Peer Pressure, Relationships
Genres: Realistic
Awards: 2006 Printz
Lists: 2006 BBYA, 2006 QP
Levels: PW 9 up, SLJ 9 up

Annotation: Miles, fascinated with famous last words, enters the Alabama boarding school his father had attended, becomes part of a close group of friends, and falls in love with Alaska, a mentally unstable older girl.

Booktalk: Mild-mannered Miles Halter is fascinated with people's last words. His favorite has to do with what a dying poet called "The Great Perhaps." Miles was off to find his own great perhaps at the same prep school in Alabama that his father had attended. What Miles wasn't expecting was to fall in love with Alaska. Not the state, but one messed up, funny, clever, and downright sexy upperclassman. Oops, classwoman. Alaska knows how Miles feels about her and plays into his feelings, getting him to go along with escapades that she and his roommate Chip, called the Colonel, mastermind. Miles is happy to follow along with the antics so he can be close to Alaska. Even the possibility of getting kicked out of school his first semester there isn't enough to scare Miles away from her. Alaska is hardly a good influence on Miles. But then again, who says that everyone who has an enormous impact on your life, forcing you to start becoming who you will be in your own great perhaps, has to be? Certainly not Miles.

Excerpt: Page 13 to break on page 16.

Curriculum Connections: Creative Writing, English
Schedule time in the library media center for students to research people in the news. Based on their research, have students write what they think might be a particular person's last words, discussing why they chose these words in relation to that person's life.

Similar Titles:
Green, John, *An Abundance of Katherines.* Dutton, 2006, 256pp. $16.99. ISBN: 0525476881.
Hautman, Pete, *Rash.* Simon & Schuster, 2006, 256pp. $15.95. ISBN: 0689868014.
Knowles, John, *A Separate Peace.* Scribner, 1996, 208pp. $21. ISBN: 0684833662. Scribner, 2003, 208pp. $10. ISBN: 0743253973.
Nelson, Blake, *The New Rules of High School.* Viking, 2003, 256pp. $16.99. ISBN: 0670036447. Puffin, 2004, 240pp. $6.99. ISBN: 0142402427.
Weaver, Will, *Full Service.* Farrar, Straus & Giroux, 2005, 240pp. $17. ISBN: 0374324859.

Hartinger, Brent, *The Last Chance Texaco.* 41

HarperCollins, 2004, 240pp. $15.99. ISBN: 0060509120. HarperCollins, 2005, 240pp. $6.99. ISBN: 0060509147.
Web Site: <www.brenthartinger.com>
Subjects: Bullying, Emotional Problems, Fires, Foster Homes, High Schools, Native Americans, Orphans, Prejudices, Relationships, Self-Esteem
Genres: Mystery, Realistic
Lists: 2005 QP, 2006 PP
Levels: BL 6-10, LMC 7-10, PW 9 up, SLJ 7-10

Annotation: Fifteen-year-old foster teen Lucy knows she is gone too far and that her new group home is the last stop before she is sent to the high security facility called Eat-Their-Young-Island. The staff, especially Leon, the Native-American counselor, and the couple who run the home, Ben and Gina, help Lucy deal with her anger.

Booktalk: Did you ever notice that some people don't realize they "hate" something or someone because they don't understand it or know anything about them? The rich teens in the area where Kindle House, a group home for teens, is located hate having the teens from the group home in their neighborhood and high school. They don't understand how someone who once lived in their nice neighborhood could donate their home to be used for housing these throw-away kids. That's what Nate thinks until Lucy slugs him in the face for one for his nasty comments in class. Because of their altercation, Nate and Lucy end up on garbage detail together. As they collect trash and talk, Lucy helps change Nate's impression of "groupies," what the rich kids call the teens in the group home. Lucy and Nate's tentative friendship slowly becomes romantic and together they try to save Kindle House, what the residents call the Last Chance Texaco, from being closed down. The homeowners in the area want Kindle House closed down because of the mysterious fires being set in the neighborhood. Lucy doesn't want to be sent to the high security juvenile facility. Kindle House is her last chance before being sent there. The result of their investigation proves to be flammable.

Excerpt: First full paragraph on page 5 through page 11.

Curriculum Connections: Geography, History, Sociology
Schedule time in the library media center for students to research the history of neighborhoods in their town to determine if the demographics and cultural make-up of the residents in these areas have changed, discussing how the original residents may have felt about the changes.

Similar Titles:
Frost, Helen, ***Keesha's House.*** Farrar, Straus & Giroux, 2003, 128pp. $16. ISBN: 0374340641. Farrar, Straus & Giroux, 2007, 128pp. $8. ISBN: 0374400121.
Gibbons, Kaye, ***The Life All Around Me by Ellen Foster.*** Harcourt, 2005, 224pp. $23. ISBN: 0151012040. Harcourt, 2006, 240pp. $13. ISBN: 0156032902. Random House Audio, 2005, $29.95. CD. ISBN: 0739321900.
Krebs, Betsy, ***Beyond the Foster Care System: The Future for Teens.*** Rutgers University Press, 2006, 238pp. $23.95. ISBN: 0813538289.
Rapp, Adam, ***The Buffalo Tree.*** Front Street, 2007, 188pp. $10.95. ISBN: 1932425993.
Sparks, Beatrice, ***Finding Katie: The Diary of Anonymous, a Teenager in Foster Care.*** Avon, 2005, 192pp. $5.99. ISBN: 0060507217.

Hartinger, Brent, *The Order of the Poison Oak.*
HarperCollins, 2005. $16.89. ISBN: 0060567317. HarperCollins, 2006, 240pp. $6.99. ISBN: 0060567325.

Web Site: <www.brenthartinger.com>
Subjects: Body Image, Disabilities, Emotional Problems, Fires, Friendship, Homosexuality, Peer Pressure, Self-Esteem, Summer Camps
Genres: Realistic
Levels: BL 7-10, SLJ 8 up

Annotation: Sixteen-year-old Russell takes a job at a summer camp for burn victims to get away from being harassed at school after coming out about being gay and learns about life from a group of 10-year-old boys.

Booktalk: Have you ever met one of those beautiful people who, once you got to know them, turned out to be nothing but an empty shell? Just because something is beautiful on the outside does not mean it is beautiful on the inside. Russell found that out about Web, one of the other counselors at the summer camp for burn victims where they are working. Unlike Web, who is nothing but eye candy, the 10-year-old boys who Russell works with aren't pretty to look at, but they are one smart group of kids. They have the depth of feeling and empathy that Web will never have, nor could understand. Russell begins to understand this and care for his unruly charges after he figures out how to get them under control. At first he is afraid to discipline them because they are burn victims, but their antics remind him, loud and clear, that they really are just a group of rowdy boys who know they can manipulate Russell and get away with doing things they never would have otherwise. But Russell learns how to gain their respect and they engage in a special ceremony that bonds them as a group. But what Russell gives them at the ceremony almost results in the death of one of them.

Excerpt: Page 31 to break on page 39.

Curriculum Connections: Biology, Health, Science
Russell's campers are a group of boys who have suffered serious burns. Schedule time in the library media center for students to research facilities and new medical procedures that are available to assist in the healing process of burn victims.

Similar Titles:
Crutcher, Chris, *Staying Fat for Sarah Byrnes.* Greenwillow, 1993, 224pp. $17.99. ISBN: 0688115527. HarperCollins, 2003, 295pp. $6.99. ISBN: 0060094893.
Gideon, Melanie, *Pucker.* Razorbill, 2006, 288pp. $16.99. ISBN: 1595140557.
Hartinger, Brent, *Geography Club.* HarperCollins, 2003, 226pp. $16.99. ISBN: 0060012218. HarperCollins, 2004, 226pp. $6.99. ISBN: 0060012234.
Hartinger, Brent, *Grand and Humble.* HarperCollins, 2006, 213pp. $15.99. ISBN: 0060567279.

Sanchez, Alex, ***Rainbow High.*** Simon & Schuster, 2003, 247pp. $16.95. ISBN: 0689854773. Simon & Schuster, 2005, 272pp. $8.99. ISBN: 0689854781.

43 Hautman, Pete, *Invisible.*

Simon & Schuster, 2005, 160pp. $15.95. ISBN: 068988006. Simon & Schuster, 2006, 160pp. $7.99. ISBN: 0689869037.

Web Site: <www.petehautman.com>
Subjects: Accidents, Bullying, Death, Depression, Emotional Problems, Fires, Friendship, Grieving, High Schools, Mental Illness
Genres: Realistic, Suspense
Lists: 2006 BBYA
Levels: BL 7-10, K 6-12, PW 6 up, SLJ 7 up, V 7-12

Annotation: After his best friend's death in a fire, 17-year-old Doug Hanson, a target of ridicule at school, has been building model train cities to try to forget his role in the fire but Andy keeps appearing and bringing back the painful memories.

Booktalk: Doug Hanson has it about as bad as it can be as a geeky guy in high school. He gets beat up by the other guys and the girl of his dreams calls him a worm. It doesn't help his case any that he just sits there and stares at her in class. Plain and simple, he creeps her out. To tell you the truth, he'd creep me out too if he stared at me like that. She'd be doing a lot more than calling him Worm if she knew that Doug sneaks out at night and climbs a tree near her house and waits for when she turns on her bedroom light to get ready for bed. After his Peeping Tom episodes, his best friend Andy is waiting for him when he gets back home and tells Doug he is going to get caught. Andy is Doug's next door neighbor and they have been best friends since they were little kids. Doug and Andy still hang out and talk between their bedroom windows like they did before IT happened, but Doug does not want to talk about what happened to them a few years ago. He *won't* talk about it and he tries not to even think about IT. When IT starts to creep up in his mind he goes down to the basement and builds. He builds something new for his model train landscape that now covers two ping pong tables. All of it is built out of wooden matchsticks. Doug meticulously scrapes the heads off of the matches so they can't ignite. Doug doesn't like to think about what matches and flames can do. He tries to lose himself in his trains and become *Invisible.*

Excerpt: Chapter 6.

Curriculum Connections: Art, History
Doug has been working on a sigil, sometimes described as a symbol or signet whose purpose is known only to the creator. Schedule time in the library media center for students to research the history of sigils and to design one for themselves or their family.

Similar Titles:
Hautman, Pete, *Mr. Was.* Simon Pulse, 1998, 256pp. $5.99. ISBN: 0689819145.
Johnson, Kathleen Jeffrie, *A Fast and Brutal Wing.* Roaring Brook, 2004, 192pp. $16.95. ISBN: 1596430133.
Mental Health Information for Teens: Health Tips About Mental Wellness and Mental Illness: Including Facts About Mental and Emotional Health, Depression and Other Mood Disorders, Anxiety Disorders, Behavior Disorders, Self-Injury, Psychosis. Omnigraphics, 2006, 400pp. $65. ISBN: 0780808630.
Schiller, Lori, *The Quiet Room: A Journey Out of the Torment of Madness.* Warner, 1996, 288pp. $13.95. ISBN: 446671339.
Vizzini, Ned, *Be More Chill.* Miramax, 2004, 304pp. $16.95. ISBN: 0786809957. Miramax, 2005, 304pp. $7.99. ISBN: 0786809965. HarperCollinsAudio, 2004, $27.95. CD. ISBN: 0060747811.

44

Hearn, Julie, *The Minister's Daughter.*

Simon & Schuster, 2005, 272pp. $16.95. ISBN: 0689876904. Simon Pulse, 2006, 272pp. $7.99. ISBN: 0689876912. Listening Library, 2005, $37. ISBN: 0307245489.

Web Site: <www.julie-hearn.com>
Subjects: Emotional Problems, Fairies, Fathers and Daughters, Magic, Medicine, Occupations, Pregnancy, Prejudices, Religion, Sexual Relationships, Sisters, Witchcraft
Genres: Fantasy, Historical, International, Religious, Supernatural
Lists: 2006 BBYA
Levels: BL 7-10, PW 6 up, SLJ 7 up

Annotation: Nell, an herb gatherer and healer in 1645 England, is proclaimed a witch by Grace, the manipulative Puritan minister's daughter who is faking an illness and bizarre behavior to hide her pregnancy after Nell refuses to terminate it.

Booktalk: Nell lives in a time when healers and herb gatherers can, in the time it takes for a nasty rumor to leave someone's lips, go from being sought after midwives to hated witches, with just an accusation or two. When Nell is summoned to the parsonage but refuses to help the minister's daughter Grace out of her predicament, she accuses Nell of witchcraft. Grace has been involved in late night activities very unbecoming of a minister's daughter and has decided to focus blame for her condition elsewhere. Poor Nell has no idea how manipulative a minister's daughter can be when she is no longer able to hide the results of her secret trysts with one of the village men. No one suspects Grace, a minister's daughter, of doing anything immoral. And, of course, she cannot be faking her bizarre behavior because her sister is acting strangely too. Besides, they are the pious daughters of the local minister. They must have been bewitched and poor Nell is blamed for Grace's "demonic" behavior. Nell is the perfect target. She and her befuddled grandmother are witches, aren't they? No matter that they have helped heal many of the villagers and delivered most of their babies. No questions asked. Of course they are witches—the minister's daughter says so.

Excerpt: Pages 104 through 106.

Curriculum Connections: History, Psychology
Part of the novel is set during the Salem Witch Trials, from the perspective of Patience, Grace's younger sister, who went along with Grace's deception. Schedule time in the library media center for students to research the Salem Witch Trials and the accusations made by young girls, discussing the similarities between what happened to Nell and in Salem.

Similar Titles:
Aronson, Marc, ***Witch-Hunts: Mysteries of the Salem Witch Trials.*** Atheneum, 2003, 228pp. $18.95. ISBN: 0689848641. Simon Pulse, 2005, 288pp. $8.99. ISBN: 1416903151.
Bunn, Ivan, ***A Trial of Witches.*** Routledge, 1997, 284pp. $70. ISBN: 0415171083. Routledge, 1997, 304pp. $40.95. ISBN: 0415171091.
Jordan, Sherryl, ***The Raging Quiet.*** Simon Pulse, 2004, 362pp. $5.99. ISBN: 0689870043.
Napoli, Donna Jo, ***The Magic Circle.*** Puffin, 1995, 128pp. $4.99. ISBN: 0140374396.
Rinaldi, Ann, ***A Break with Charity: A Story about the Salem Witch Trials.*** Harcourt, 1992, 257pp. $17. ISBN: 0152003533. Harcourt, 2003, 320pp. $6.95. ISBN: 0152046828.

45 Hoffman, Alice, *Green Angel.*

Scholastic, 2003, 128pp. $14.95. ISBN: 0439443849. Scholastic, 2004, 128pp. $5.99. ISBN: 0439443857.

Web Site: <www.alicehoffman.com>
Subjects: Death, Depression, Dogs, Elderly, Emotional Problems, Fires, Friendship, Grieving, Sisters, Survival
Genres: Science Fiction
Levels: BL 6-12, PW 6 up, SLJ 8 up

Annotation: Sparse lyrical prose tells the story of 15-year-old Green who lives a quiet country life with her family until her parents and little sister are killed in an apocalyptic fire that leaves her alone to fend off looters and to deal with her grief and loneliness, until she is befriended by a dog, a lost boy, and an elderly woman.

Booktalk: Did you ever wonder what your guardian angels might look like if the world as you know it came to a violent end? What if one minute the sky was blue and the next the horizon was red with flames and ash was falling thickly to the ground? In this novel angels appear in the most unique shapes and forms. Green needs guardian angels to help pull her out of the self-destructive depression she sinks into when her parents and little sister die in an apocalyptic fire. Green doesn't believe she is the daughter worthy of having survived. She doesn't want to be herself anymore and renames herself Ash. To ensure she becomes the dark creature she wants to be, Ash begins to build her self-protective armor by adding nails to her boots, thorns to her dad's leather jacket, and inks tattoos of a raven and thorns onto her body. Green is disappearing into her alter ego Ash. But guardian angels in the form of a pure white greyhound, a mute boy, and an elderly woman help her rise from the Ash of her grief to become Green again. Where does she go from here?

Excerpt: From break on page 7 to break on page 11.

Curriculum Connections: History, Science
Schedule time in the library media center for students to research the great fires of the past and determine how plants and animals indigenous to the area adapted, as well as the human response to these tragic fires.

Similar Titles:
Butler, Octavia E., *The Parable of the Sower.* Warner Brothers, 1995, 304pp. $6.99. ISBN: 0446601977.
Hoffman, Alice, *The Foretelling.* Little Brown, 2006, 176pp. $16.95. ISBN: 0316010189. Little Brown, 2006, 192pp. $7.99. ISBN: 0316154091.
McDevitt, Jack, *Eternity Road.* HarperCollins, 1998, 416pp. $7.99. ISBN: 0061054275.
Rosoff, Meg, *How I Live Now.* Random House, 2004, 208pp. $16.95. ISBN: 0385746776. Random House, 2005, 224pp. $7.99. ISBN: 0553376055. Random House Audio, 2005, $28. CD. ISBN: 0307281841.
Westerfeld, Scott, *The Last Days.* Penguin, 2006, 320pp. $16.99. ISBN: 159514062X.

Hoffman, Alice, *Incantation.*

Little Brown, 2006, 166pp. $16.99. ISBN: 0316010197. Brilliance Audio, 2006, $44.25. ISBN: 1423323587. Brilliance Audio, 2006, $62.25. CD. ISBN: 14233233602.

Web Site: <www.alicehoffman.com>
Subjects: Brothers and Sisters, Censorship, Death, Elderly, Family Problems, Fires, Friendship, Grandparents, Grieving, Jealousy, Jews, Journeys, Medicine, Mothers and Daughters, Murder, Prejudices, Relationships, Religion, Survival, Violence
Genres: Historical, International, Religious, Romance
Levels: KL 6-12, PW 6 up, SLJ 7 up

Annotation: Sixteen-year-old Estrella discovers that her mother, brother, and grandparents are Jewish, but the family is hiding as devout Catholics during the Inquisition in Spain during the 1500s.

Booktalk: Estrella and her best friend since childhood, Catalina, had done everything together. They were sure that they would marry and live right next door to each other just as they always have. Their husbands would be best friends and their children would be raised together. These wonderful innocent dreams of the future would be shattered by jealousy. Catalina was betrothed to her cousin Andres, but love doesn't always follow the rules and Andres falls in love with Estrella. At first Catalina does not realize what is really happening and merely warns Estrella to stay away from Andres, but when she discovers they have been secretly meeting, Catalina's jealousy becomes deadly. She had always teased Estrella about the strange manner in which her family did things, including how they crossed themselves in church, but the teasing turned deadly when a list of ways to determine if someone is a Jew appears as a posted decree, with a reward for those who turn them in. Catalina and Estrella both read the decree and realized a truth about Estrella's family that neither had known before. And, while Catalina plotted revenge, Estrella feared for her family's safety, realizing her entire life had been based on a lie. A lie that Catalina now knows and can use against her rival for Andres.

Excerpt: From the paragraph beginning at the bottom of page 64 to break on page 68.

Curriculum Connections: History
Estrella's family were Marranos, Spanish Jews who lived a double life pretending to be devout Catholics while practicing the Kabbalah in secret. Schedule time in the library media center for students to research the Marranos during the Inquisition period in Spain and discuss how they were able to keep their identities hidden.

Similar Titles:
Gordon, Noah, ***The Last Jew.*** St. Martin's Press, 2002, 352pp. $14.95. ISBN: 0312300530. St. Martin's Press, 2001, 352pp. $6.99. ISBN: 0312978391.
Gregory, Philippa, ***The Queen's Fool.*** Simon & Schuster, 2004, 512pp. $22.95. ISBN: 0743269829. Simon & Schuster, 2005, 512pp. $16. ISBN: 0641733240.
Lasky, Kathryn, ***Blood Secret.*** HarperCollins, 2004, 256pp. $16.89. ISBN: 0060000651. HarperTrophy, 2006, 304pp. $5.99. ISBN: 0060000635.
Paris, Erna, ***The End of Days: A Story of Tolerance, Tyranny and the Expulsion of Jews from Spain.*** Prometheus, 1995, 327pp. $39. ISBN: 1573920177.
Siegel, Deborah Spector, ***The Cross by Day, the Mezzuzah by Night.*** Jewish Publication Society, 2000, 213pp. $9.95. ISBN: 0827607377.

Hooper, Mary, *Amy.*
Bloomsbury, 2002, 176pp. $14.95. ISBN: 158234793X. Bloomsbury, 2004, 176pp. $6.95. ISBN: 1582349150.

Web Site: <www.maryhooper.co.uk>
Subjects: Crime, Emotional Problems, Friendship, High Schools, Sexual Assault, Writing
Genres: International, Realistic
Levels: BL 9-12, K 6-10, PW 5 up, SLJ 7 up

Annotation: Fifteen-year-old Amy feels left out when her girlfriends stop doing things with her so she finds solace on the Internet by chatting with Zed who says he is 18. Amy goes on a picnic with him to the British seashore where he drugs her and takes nude photographs. Amy narrates the incident via a conversation with the police and the chat room transcript.

Booktalk: Maybe I got sick because I was so nervous about meeting him in person for the first time. I was worried he wouldn't like me even though we had been talking online for weeks. Maybe I had too much to eat or maybe it was something I ate. But Zed didn't get sick and we ate the same thing, except for the mousse. I had chocolate and he had lemon. It isn't like me to fall asleep at the beach, but I felt sick to my stomach and so sleepy that I must have just fallen asleep. I was so embarrassed by throwing up when I first woke up that I tried to cover it up with sand. Can being in the sun for too long make you dizzy and sick? I still feel yucky and kind of weird, like something happened that shouldn't have. I made it past Mum and Dad without too much trouble but now that I am in my room I just want to get out of my sandy clothes and into bed. Hey, wait a minute, the tag is in the front on my tank top. How did that happen? I put it on the right way this morning, didn't I? Did something happen at the beach that I don't remember?

Excerpt: Second paragraph on page 12 to end of first paragraph on page 14.

Curriculum Connections: English, History
Schedule time in the library media center for students to research other forms of abbreviated communication such as those used in online chat rooms. Have small groups create a message that integrates at least two different abbreviated forms of communication, along with a basic key to decipher the code. Have groups exchange the messages for decoding.

Similar Titles:
Cray, Jordan, ***Gemini 7. Danger.com.*** Aladdin, 1997, 190pp. $3.99. ISBN: 0689814321.
Doherty, Berlie, ***Holly Starcross.*** HarperCollins, 2002, 192pp. $15.99. ISBN: 0060013419.
MacDonald, Joan Vos, ***Cybersafety: Surfing Safely Online.*** Enslow, 2001, 64pp. $17.95. ISBN: 0766015807.

Power, Ashley, ***Goosehead Guide to Life.*** Hyperion, 2001, 150pp. $14.99. ISBN: 0786815817.

Tarbox, Katherine, ***A Girl's Life Online.*** Plume, 2004, 192pp. $14. ISBN: 0452286611.

48 Hopkins, Ellen, *Burned.*

Simon & Schuster, 2006, 529pp. $16.95. ISBN: 1416903542. Simon Pulse, 2007, 384pp. $8.99. ISBN: 1416903550.

Web Site: <www.ellenhopkins.com>
Subjects: Accidents, Alcohol Abuse, Body Image, Child Abuse, Emotional Problems, Family Problems, Fathers and Daughters, Journeys, Relationships, Religion, Sexual Relationships
Genres: Poetry, Realistic, Religious
Levels: BL 9-12, SLJ 9 up, V 10-12

Annotation: Seventeen-year-old Pattyn wants to do things other teenage girls in her Utah high school do, but most are not allowed by her abusive Mormon father, including spending time with boys rather than taking care of her little brothers and sisters. Pattyn is sent to live with her aunt when her father catches her with a boy. Written in verse.

Booktalk: Do things that are supposed to be taboo sound interesting to you? That is certainly the case for Pattyn, the oldest daughter in a large Mormon family ruled by the iron fist of a military minded father. He is military to the core—Pattyn is even named after one of his favorite generals. The environment at home is less than relaxing for Pattyn even though her mother calmly takes the verbal and physical abuse her father regularly administers. Her mother's refusal to stand up for herself frustrates Pattyn. Her mother continues to have baby after baby, but she can't keep up with taking care of all of them. Pattyn is the one taking care of the little ones most of the time. A social life of her own? What's that? So when Pattyn's father teaches her how to target practice she finds the repetitive loading and shooting action soothing and gets very good at it as now she has an excuse to get away from the house. She is out in the desert target practicing when a group of guys from school come by on their 4-wheelers and she catches Derek's attention. Before long they are secretly meeting out in the desert. That is until her father catches them and threatens Derek with what he will do to him if he even talks to his daughter again. But, the damage has been done. Pattyn is questioning everything in her life—her religion, her family beliefs, and her self-worth. You know, it can be said that one's heart screams in poetry. Listen to Pattyn's heart in *Burned*.

Excerpt: Page 50 through page 56.

Curriculum Connections: Creative Writing, English
Hopkins has employed a variety of poetry formats to convey Pattyn's feelings and to describe her life. Schedule time in the library media center for students to explore

poetry collections of various poetic styles, such as free verse and concrete poems. Have students choose one of the styles and write a poem they would share with Pattyn.

Similar Titles:
Hobbs, Valerie, ***How Far Would You Have Gotten If I Hadn't Called You Back?*** Scholastic, 2003, 320pp. $6.99. ISBN: 0439583969.
Hopkins, Ellen, ***Crank.*** Simon Pulse, 2004, 544pp. $8.99. ISBN: 0689865198.
Hopkins, Ellen, ***Impulse.*** Simon & Schuster, 2007, 672pp. $16.99. ISBN: 1416903569.
Hughes, Dean, ***Soldier Boys.*** Atheneum, 2001, 259pp. $16.95. ISBN: 0689817487. Simon Pulse, 2003, 240pp. $5.99. ISBN: 0689860218.
Na, An, ***A Step from Heaven.*** Boyds Mills, 2001, 156pp. $16.95. ISBN: 886910588. Penguin, 2002, 160pp. $7.99. ISBN: 0142500275.

Jones, Patrick, *Nailed.*
Walker, 2006, 216pp. $16.95. ISBN: 0802780776. Walker, 2007, 240pp. $7.95. ISBN: 0802796486.

49

Web Site: <www.connectingya.com>
Subjects: Acting, Body Image, Bullying, Family Problems, Fathers and Sons, Friendship, High Schools, Music, Peer Pressure, Self-Esteem
Genres: Realistic
Levels: BL 9-12, PW 9 up, SLJ 9 up

Annotation: Sixteen-year-old Bret, with his long purple tinted hair and baggy clothes, loves acting and music but does not allow himself to fit in at home with his sports and cars-oriented father or at school where he gets bullied.

Booktalk: Yes, nonviolence is good, but by not standing up for himself, ever, nonconformist Bret gets nailed, frequently. Sometimes the harassment is physical, but he deals with it. That's just the way he is. Bret's life revolves around quietly rebelling against his angry father, getting through the school day, and relaxing by playing music with his buddies Alex and Sean. Then the petite and worldly Kylee turns his world upside down when they work together on a play. Kylee is rebelling in her own way and decides she will be the center of Bret's world. They are inseparable until she gets bored with him when he has more to do with his life than spend every waking moment with her. So Kylee dumps him and callously moves on to her next conquest, his best friend Sean. Bret might be brokenhearted, but he isn't through rebelling and his speech before the student body results in ACLU involvement. It isn't until Bret and Alex step out on the loading dock behind the school during the Prom and discover they are not alone that Bret finally realizes it is time to stand up for himself.

Excerpt: Page 5 through page 6.

Curriculum Connections: English, Psychology, Sociology
When Bret asks Kylee if she knows what it means to be normal, she asks why anyone would want to be normal. Schedule time in the library media center for students to explore societal definitions of normal and how these definitions relate to a person's ability to fit into social groups, and discuss what is considered normal in their school environment.

Similar Titles:
Cohn, Rachel and David Levithan, ***Nick and Norah's Infinite Playlist.*** Random House, 2006, 192pp. $16.95. ISBN: 0375835318.
Cormier, Robert, ***The Chocolate War.*** Random House, 1997, 264pp. $16.95. ISBN: 0394828054. Random House, 1986, 272pp. $6.99. ISBN: 0440944597. Random House Audio, 2004, $26. ISBN: 1400085330.
Jones, Patrick, ***Chasing Tail Lights.*** Walker, 2007, 304pp. $16.95. ISBN: 0802796281.
Jones, Patrick, ***Things Change.*** Walker, 2004, 216pp. $16.95. ISBN: 0802789013. Walker, 2006, 228pp. $7.95. ISBN: 0802777465.
Thomas, Rob, ***Rats Saw God.*** Simon & Schuster, 1996, 224pp. $17. ISBN: 0689802072. Simon Pulse, 1996, 202pp. $5.99. ISBN: 0689807775.

50 Kennen, Ally, *Beast.*

Scholastic, 2006, 217pp. $16.99. ISBN: 0439865492.
Web Site: <www.allykennen.com>
Subjects: Animals, Crocodiles, Fathers and Sons, Foster Homes, Stress, Violence
Genres: International, Mystery, Realistic, Suspense
Levels: SLJ 8 up

Annotation: Seventeen-year-old Stephen, who has lived in foster homes much of his life, has been feeding a crocodile his ex-con father gave to him as a pet that Stephen put in a cage-like structure next to a reservoir four years ago. While trying to move the now very large and dangerous animal to a stronger cage, it escapes.

Booktalk: I been living with the Reynolds for three years now and it really isn't so bad, except for that Carol. Never trust a girl who wears pink. When her mum or dad is around Carol is all sweet and girlie, but when they are gone, she is wicked. I call her Daughter of Satan. She spends her free time figuring out new ways to get me in trouble or make my life miserable. I try to ignore her, but that doesn't usually work. So, of course, it has to be Carol who sees the light on in her dad's garden shed. I knew it was risky to take the chance of doing it at the house, but I couldn't carry something that heavy by myself and I sure couldn't get it over the fence in one piece. So I was in the shed, cutting it up into pieces. It was a messy job and I had blood all over me when I saw movement and looked up to find Carol in the doorway. She looked at me all wide eyed and her voice wobbled when she told me that I was all covered in blood. She wanted to know what I was doing while I tried to stop her from going into the shed. She forced her way past me and then started screaming, "Murder!" They didn't give me a chance. When Carol's dad asked who she was I told him just a pig. That really made him mad. He thought I had cut up some girl with a hacksaw in his shed and I was calling her a pig. It took me awhile to make him understand it really was a pig's carcass I was cutting up. Took me less time to convince him that I was cutting it up to bring to my dad, and that was the lie. I was taking it out to the Beast. It had been awhile since I fed him and I knew he was hungry. I shuddered to think of the roar I would hear when he smelled me coming through the woods with his dinner.

Excerpt: From break on page 19 through page 22.

Curriculum Connections: Biology, Geography, Science
Eric tells Stephen that England's climate is too cold for a crocodile to survive the winter. Schedule time in the library media center for students to research crocodiles and the weather in countries to which crocodiles are native, comparing their temperatures to England's and discuss the validity of Eric's assumption that a crocodile could not survive an English winter.

Similar Titles:
de la Pena, Matt, ***Ball Don't Lie.*** Random House, 2005, 288pp. $16.95. ISBN: 0385732325.
Fleischman, Paul, ***Breakout.*** Cricket, 2003, 160pp. $15.95. ISBN: 0812626966.
Simon & Schuster, 2005, 144pp. $6.99. ISBN: 0689871899.
Garlock, Michael, ***Killer 'Gators and Crocs: Gruesome Encounters from Across the Globe.*** Lyon Press, 2006, 232pp. $14.95. ISBN: 1592289754.
Martel, Yann, ***Life of Pi.*** Harcourt, 2002, 336pp. $25. ISBN: 0151008116. Harcourt, 2003, 348pp. $14. ISBN: 0156027321. Highbridge Audio, 2003, $36.95. CD. ISBN: 1565117808.
Rottman, S.L., ***Rough Waters.*** Peachtree, 1998, 192pp. $14.95. ISBN: 156145172X. Puffin, 2000, 256pp. $6.99. ISBN: 014130703X.

Klass, David, *Firestorm.*

The Caretaker Trilogy, Farrar, Straus & Giroux, 2006, 304pp. $17. ISBN: 0374323070.

Subjects: Animals, Body Image, Death, Dogs, Ecology, Fathers and Sons, Football, Genetics, Journeys, Medical Experimentation, Murder, Oceans, Survival, Teachers, Time Travel
Genres: Adventure, Science Fiction, Suspense
Levels: KL 6–12, PW 5 up, SLJ 8 up

Annotation: Eighteen-year-old Jack discovers he has been sent from the future to save the world from man's destruction of the Earth's natural resources, especially the oceans from reef destruction by fishing boats, with the help of a female mentor and a talking dog.

Booktalk: Let me tell you about myself. My name is Jack Danielson. Pretty normal name, right? I thought I was a typical high school guy with the typical hobbies: chicks, flicks, and fast cars. In that order. Oh yeah, and sports. Left that out, but I am a natural at sports. I'm the starting running back on the football team. Of course I am. I'm 6'2" and of above average brain power. Oh yeah, and I have a winning smile. That smile is for P.J. Peters, my girlfriend. So, in other words, I lived a pretty normal high school jock's life. Then this strange guy shows up in the diner when P.J. and I were eating after the winning football game. He stood there and just stared at me. He didn't look at anyone else, just me. What a weird looking guy; gangly and tall with an Adam's apple sticking out so far in front of his neck that I wanted to pluck it. This part you aren't going to believe but it's true. He stared at me and then his eyes rolled back in his head and when they reappeared there were no pupils, just a burst of white light. Only problem is, no one saw this happen but me. Matter of fact, no one else even saw the guy in the diner. And that's when my days of flirting with P.J. and playing football ended. Later that night I found out that my father is from the future and was sent here to protect me. But now he's dead. I saw him fall to the pavement when they shot him as he tried to protect me. I'm on the run, chased by the same kind of guys as the one I saw in the diner. The same guys that shot my dad. Dad said they are after me because I am the last hope for this planet. I am *Firestorm*, whatever that is.

Excerpt: Chapter 3.

Curriculum Connections: Biology, Geography, Science
Firestorm is the only YA title that Greenpeace International has ever endorsed on their Web site: <www.greenpeace.org/international/photosvideos/audios/firestorm>. Schedule time in the library media center for students to visit the Greenpeace International Web site, as well as others related to bottom trawlers, and discuss what this type of fishing does to ocean reefs.

Similar Titles:
Glover, Linda K., ***Defying Ocean's End: An Agenda for Action.*** Island Press, 2004, 283pp. $30. ISBN: 1559637552.
Gore, Al, ***An Inconvenient Truth: The Crisis of Global Warming.*** Penguin, 2007, 92pp. $23. ISBN: 0670062715. Penguin, 2007, 192pp. $16.99. ISBN: 0670062723.
Klass, David, ***California Blue.*** Scholastic, 1996, 208pp. $5.99. ISBN: 0590466895.
Patterson, James, ***Maximum Ride: The Angel Experiment.*** Little Brown, 2005, 432pp. $16.95. ISBN: 031615556X. Warner, 2006, 464pp. $6.99. ISBN: 0446617792.
Woodard, Colin, ***Ocean's End: Travels Through Endangered Seas.*** Basic Books, 2001, 300pp. $15. ISBN: 0465015719.

Klause, Annette Curtis, *Freaks: Alive on the Inside!*
Simon & Schuster, 2006, 331pp. $16.95. ISBN: 068987037X.

Web Site: <www.childrensbookguild.org/klause.htm>
Subjects: Body Image, Circuses, Disabilities, Friendship, Genetics, Journeys, Magic, Mummies, Prejudices, Runaways, Sexual Relationships
Genres: Fantasy, Historical, Supernatural
Levels: BL 10-12, K 6-10, KL 10-12, PW 9 up, SLJ 9 up

Annotation: Seventeen-year-old Abel Dandy grew up in Fairyland, a Midwest freak show, but runs away to join the circus in 1899, where he thinks he will become a famous knife thrower, but instead falls in love with an Egyptian mummy who is slowly coming to life.

Booktalk: I'll just say it! Abel Dandy is a teenage guy who is not above kissing the dog-faced girl for a thrill. But as a "normal human" with no physical abnormalities he doesn't fit in at the freak show he has lived in all of his life. Abel decides to make a name for himself in a "regular" circus but discovers that his knife throwing skills aren't a big deal there either. Maybe his throwing skills aren't improving because he is having sexy dreams about an Egyptian woman. He can't seem to concentrate on much of anything else, especially after discovering that the scarab ring, given to him by one of the Siamese twins when they left the freak show, is no ordinary ring. When Abel puts the ring on, it slowly brings the Egyptian woman he is dreaming about to life. Her mummy is one of the displays in the circus he joins. In a gross out kind of way, her mummy coming to life because of him is making his physical desire even stronger. Now don't get me wrong. Although Abel sounds a bit weird, he is also just a regular nice guy who goes out of his way to help everyone, including the little dog-faced boy who follows him to the circus. After all, it was his older sister who Abel kissed, so he felt obligated. But helping a mummy who wants to comes to life? I think that is a bit weird. Don't you wonder what Abel will do with her once her transformation is complete?

Excerpt: Page 6 through page 10.

Curriculum Connections: History
Have students reread the Author's Note at the end of the book, choosing one of the real life figures or places Klause addresses. Schedule time in the library media center for student to research their chosen topic and to later share what they learned with the class.

Similar Titles:
Fleischman, Paul, *Whirligig.* Holt, 1998, 133pp. $16.95. ISBN: 0805055827. Random House, 1999, 144pp. $5.99. ISBN: 0440228352. Audio Bookshelf, 1999, $24.95. ISBN: 1883332389. Audio Bookshelf, 2000, $29.95. CD. ISBN: 1883332699.

Hartzman, Marc, ***American Sideshow: An Encyclopedia of History's Most Wondrous and Curiously Strange Performers.*** Tarcher, 2005, 304pp. $28.95. ISBN: 1585424412.

Klause, Annette Curtis, ***Blood and Chocolate.*** Laurel Leaf, 1999, 288pp. $6.50. ISBN: 0440226686.

Lawrence, Iain, ***Ghost Boy.*** Random House, 2002, 352pp. $6.50. ISBN: 044041668X.

Strong, Susan, ***The Boldness of Boys: Famous Men Talk About Growing Up.*** Andrew McNeel, 2003, 251pp. $18.95. ISBN: 0740738585.

53 Lawrence, Michael, *A Crack in the Line.*

Withern Rise Trilogy. Greenwillow, 2004, 336pp. $16.89. ISBN: 0060724781. HarperCollins, 2005, 352pp. $7.99. ISBN: 006072479X.

Web Site: <www.wordybug.com>
Subjects: Accidents, Art, Death, Fathers and Sons, Grieving, Journeys, Magic, Mothers and Daughters, Mothers and Sons, Time Travel
Genres: Fantasy, International, Science Fiction
Lists: 2005 BBYA
Levels: BL 8-12, KL 6-12, PW 8 up, SLJ 7-10, V 7-12

Annotation: Sixteen-year-old British teen Alaric "accidentally" travels to an alternate reality in which his mother is still alive and befriends Naia, the girl who has taken his place as her child. Together they try to figure out what role the Family Tree plays in their ability to travel through time and they both get caught in an alternate reality.

Booktalk: Alaric remembered when his mother had ceremoniously brought him into the kitchen to unveil her work of art. She had been working on it for months. She whipped the tea towel cover off of it and dramatically proclaimed, "Behold! Lexie's Folly!" It was incredibly detailed. Under a dome of glass was a tiny wooden replica of their house. It was so true to life that one of the chimneys was slightly skewed, just like the one on the real roof. Alaric asked his mum why she called it a folly. She told him that a folly was built for fun, on a whim, or to commemorate something special. Alaric closed his eyes and remembered her delight with the end product. He hadn't looked at the folly since she died, but he was looking at it now and marveling at the accuracy and the skill that went into its creation. His need for his mother made him reach out and put his hands on the glass dome of the folly, wishing she were alive. Alaric's palms began to tingle and then there was pain so excruciating that he squeezed his eyes shut to block it out. When he was able to open his eyes he was outside in the garden, under the Family Tree. Wait a minute. There was a girl walking out of the front door of his house, acting like she lived there. He was sure it was his house, but it looked too well kept up. What was going on? Who was she? Who fixed up the house? And how did he get in the garden?

Excerpt: Page 34 through break on page 39.

Curriculum Connections: Physics, Science

Schedule time in the library media center for students to research the concept of parallel universes and discuss what the scientists and physicists theorize about the possibility of their existence.

Similar Titles:

Goodman, Alison, ***Singing the Dogstar Blues.*** Viking, 2003, 224pp. $16.99. ISBN: 0670036102. Penguin, 2004, 272pp. $6.99. ISBN: 0670036102.

Heinlein, Robert A., ***A Door into Summer.*** Random House, 1997, 304pp. $12.95. ISBN: 0345413997. Random House, 1993, 291pp. $6.99. ISBN: 0345330129. Blackstone Audio, 2006, $44.95. ISBN: 0786136782. Blackstone Audio, 2006, $55. CD. ISBN: 078617692X.

Lawrence, Michael, ***Small Eternities.*** Withern Rise Trilogy. Greenwillow, 2005, 336pp. $16.99. ISBN: 0060724803.

Lawrence, Michael, ***The Underwood See.*** Withern Rise Trilogy. Greenwillow, 2007, 224pp. $16.99. ISBN: 0060724838.

Westerfeld, Scott, ***The Secret Hour.*** The Midnighters Series. Eos, 2004, 304pp. $15.99. ISBN: 0060519517. HarperCollins, 2005, 383pp. $6.99. ISBN: 0060519533.

Lester, Julius, *Time's Memory.*

Farrar, Straus & Giroux, 2006, 232pp. $17. ISBN: 0374371784.

Web Site: <http://members.authorsguild.net/juliuslester>
Subjects: African Americans, Africans, Death, Fathers and Daughters, Ghosts, Gods and Goddesses, Grieving, Journeys, Magic, Pregnancy, Prejudices, Race Relations, Relationships, Religion, Slavery, Violence
Genres: Fantasy, Historical, Multicultural, Supernatural
Levels: BL 8-11, PW 6 up, SLJ 9 up, V 7-12

Annotation: Amina is kidnapped from her African village by slave traders and arrives in Virginia on the eve of the Civil War. She gives "birth" to Ekundayo, a Dogon spirit from Africa that her father has sent with her to save the spirits of the dead slaves. Ekundayo takes over the body of a 17-year-old slave who is in love with the plantation owner's daughter.

Booktalk: Amina's village knew the chalk-faced ones were coming and the elders were ready to welcome them, but the visitors had not come on a friendly mission. They were slave traders. Before Amina could react, her father and husband were laying on the ground with their blood running out of them like water from a hole-filled bucket. Amina crawled to them and found her husband was dead but her father was just barely breathing. She leaned over him and he reached up for her. Her father was the spiritual leader of her village and Amina thought he was going to whisper something to her. Instead, he kissed her hard on the mouth and she felt his last gasp of air enter her lungs. It wasn't until she was laying in the filth of the slave ship's hold that she felt the movement in her abdomen and heard the voice inside her head. Her father had not been kissing her in farewell, he was transferring his nyama, his spirit, to her body. And now, that spirit wanted to be brought back to life to help save the wandering nyama of the slaves who had died.

Excerpt: Chapter 2.

Curriculum Connections: Foreign Languages, Geography, History
Have students reread the Author's Note starting on page 227 before scheduling time in the library media center for students to research Mali, the Dogon people, and their language.

Similar Titles:
Azuonye, Chukwuma, ***Dogon.*** Rosen, 1996, 64pp. $15.95. ISBN: 0823919765.
Lester, Julius, ***This Strange New Feeling: Three Love Stories from Black History.*** Dial, 2006, 208pp. $16.99. ISBN: 0803731728.
Mosley, Walter, ***47.*** Little Brown, 2005, 240pp. $16.99. ISBN: 0316110353. Little Brown, 2006, 240pp. $7.99. ISBN: 0316016357. Listening Library, 2005, $30. CD. ISBN: 0307206610.
Niane, D.T., ***Sundiata: An Epic of Old Mali.*** Pearson, 2006, 128pp. $15. ISBN: 1405849428.
Taylor, Mildred, ***The Land.*** Dial, 2001, 392pp. $17.99. ISBN: 0803719507. Penguin, 2003, 375pp. $6.99. ISBN: 0142501468. Listening Library, 2001, $35. ISBN: 0807206180.

55 Mac, Carrie, *The Beckoners.*

Orca, 2004, 217pp. $16.95. ISBN: 1551433095. Orca, 2007, 217pp. $8.95. ISBN: 1551437295.

Subjects: Bullying, Emotional Problems, Friendship, Gangs, High Schools, Homosexuality, Moving, Peer Pressure, Relationships, Self-Esteem, Stress, Violence
Genres: International, Realistic
Lists: 2006 YAC
Levels: BL 8-12, K 10-12, SLJ 9 up, V 7-12

Annotation: Fifteen-year-old Zoë, a new girl in a Canadian high school, joins a vicious girl gang, gets branded at her initiation, and finds out that it was much easier to join than it is to quit when she befriends the geeky girl the gang has been tormenting.

Booktalk: The book cover shows the top of an open set of matches, deep red and ready to be stricken. And stricken they are, both the matches and the characters in this dark look into female bullying and hazing. As a new student, Zoë has no idea how feared the girl gang, the Beckoners, are. They have pretty much free rein in the school to harass anyone and April, referred to as Dog by most of the students, has been their main target for years. Other students stay away from April for fear they will come under the Beckoners' wrathful eye if they are anywhere near her, let alone help her. Before Zoë knows what it means to be a part of this group of girls, she is hanging out with the Beckoners and initiated into the gang by being branded. Zoë was in shock, but she could still smell her burning flesh and feel the intense pain. The whole initiation thing happened so fast Zoë had no idea what she was getting herself into as an official member of the Beckoners. Now that Zoë knows, she wants out. Zoë can't handle the way they treat April. It is inhuman. She won't go along with it. But there is no getting out of the Beckoners once you are in, at least not without paying for your betrayal. The Beckoners' wrath will be widespread and Zoë won't be the only one to pay.

Excerpt: Page 48 through break on page 51.

Curriculum Connections: History, Psychology, Sociology
Groups that bully and harass extend beyond high school gangs. They have been sanctioned by governments, having a tremendous impact worldwide. Have students brainstorm to create a list of bullies who have made history and schedule time in the library media center for students to research the impact these bullies, such as Hitler, have had on the people around them as well as worldwide.

Similar Titles:
Atwood, Margaret, *Cat's Eye.* Knopf, 1998, 480pp. $14.95. ISBN: 0385491026.
Blanco, Jodee, *Please Stop Laughing at Me.* Adams Media, 2003, 288pp. $12.95. ISBN: 1580628362.
Mac, Carrie, *Crush.* Orca, 2006, 112pp. $14.95. ISBN: 1551435217. Orca, 2006, 112pp. $7.95. ISBN: 1551435268.
Mayfield, Sue, *Drowning Anna.* Hyperion, 2004, 253pp. $5.99. ISBN: 0786809574.
Simmons, Rachel, *Odd Girl Speaks Out: Girls Write About Bullies, Cliques, Popularity, and Jealousy.* Harcourt, 2004, 208pp. $13. ISBN: 0156028158.

56

Meyer, Stephenie, *Twilight.*
Little Brown, 2005, 498pp. $17.99. ISBN: 0316160172. Little Brown, 2006, 544pp. $8.99. ISBN: 0316015849. Listening Library, 2005, $48. CD. ISBN: 030728090X.

Web Site: <www.stepheniemeyer.com>
Subjects: Fathers and Daughters, High Schools, Mothers and Daughters, Moving, Murder, Native Americans, Peer Pressure, Prejudices, Relationships, Vampires, Violence
Genres: Fantasy, Horror, Romance, Supernatural, Suspense
Lists: 2006 BBYA, 2006 QP
Levels: BL 9-12, KL 6-12, PW 6 up, SLJ 9 up

Annotation: Seventeen-year-old Isabella leaves sunny Phoenix and moves to the rainy Northwest to live with her father in the small town of Fork, Washington where people are friendly, but not her mysterious biology partner, who her new friends say to stay away from. But Isabella falls in love with him, loving him even after learning he is a vampire in hiding who lives on animal blood.

Booktalk: I really didn't have much choice in moving from Phoenix to live with my father. Mom married a baseball player and moved to Florida, so I ended up here with Dad in Fork, Washington, a tiny town known for breaking rainfall records. I hate the rain here. But there are some interesting changes, like my biology partner Edward Cullen. Everyone else in school has been really friendly. Not this guy. When I was assigned his lab partner he glared at me with eyes so black they looked bottomless. Bottomless pits filled with anger and hatred. I didn't think being around me was that bad but after our partner assignment he didn't show up at school for days. And when he did come back, his actions were even more confusing than his initial display of anger over being assigned my partner. Now he alternates between flirting with me, which gives me delicious shivers, to being furious with me. From day to day I never know which side of Edward Cullen I will see, but I sure prefer the flirt. I know I should dislike this guy for his weird behavior but he fascinates me. Everyone else keeps their distance from the Cullens, the five adopted teens who choose not to interact with anyone but each other while they are in school. The other Cullens are clearly not happy when Edward begins to talk to me outside of biology class. I suspected there was something very different about all of the Cullens, but when Edward saved me from being hit by a van in the school parking lot, I *knew* there was something very different about him. No human could have gotten across the parking lot that fast. He should have been hurt, if not killed, when he was hit by the van that was sliding toward me. Instead, the van has a dent in it where he held it back from hitting me. Maybe there is something to the local Native-American stories about the Cullens. I got my first piece of supporting evidence when he pushed me out of way. Edward's skin was cold to the touch.

Excerpt: First paragraph on page 18 through last paragraph on page 22.

Curriculum Connections: English, History, Psychology, Sociology
Schedule time in the school library media center for students to research Native American vampire legends, choosing different tribes' legends from which to compare similarities and differences.

Similar Titles:
Atwater-Rhodes, Amelia, **Shattered Mirror.** Bantam Doubleday Dell, 2001, 227pp. $9.95. ISBN: 0385327935. Random House, 2003, 227pp. $5.99. ISBN: 0440229405.
Bunson, Matthew, **The Vampire Encyclopedia.** Gramercy, 2000, 320pp. $7.99. ISBN: 0517162067.
Klause, Annette Curtis, **The Silver Kiss.** Random House, 1992, 216pp. $5.99. ISBN: 0440213460.

Meyer, Stephenie, **New Moon.** Little Brown, 2006, 576pp. $15.99. ISBN: 0316160199. Listening Library, 2006, $54. CD. ISBN: 0739337203.
Vande Velde, Vivian, **Companions of the Night.** Harcourt, 2002, 212pp. $5.95. ISBN: 0152166696.

Morgenroth, Kate, *Jude.*

Simon & Schuster, 2004, 277pp. $16.95. ISBN: 0689864795. Simon & Schuster, 2005, 394pp. $5.99. ISBN: 1416912673.

Subjects: Crime, Death, Drug Abuse, Emotional Problems, Fathers and Sons, Kidnapping, Mothers and Sons, Murder, Prison, Stress, Violence
Genres: Realistic
Lists: 2006 YAC
Levels: BL 9-12, KL 10 up, PW 6 up, SLJ 8 up

Annotation: After his drug dealer father is killed, 15-year-old Jude learns his mother is the District Attorney and ends up in prison for five years after being tricked to protect her political image by his mother's boyfriend, into admitting to drug dealing, which he had not done.

Booktalk: For all those years he let me think she was dead. At his side I learned how to cut cocaine and put it in baggies. Pretty interesting skill for a little kid. I was in the kitchen watching him cut cocaine the night an old buddy of his burst in and shot him. I sat at the table with my dad's killer and agreed not to tell the cops who killed him. Trouble is, the cops didn't believe my story that I had been in the living room watching TV when my dad was shot. They didn't buy the idea that I hadn't heard a thing. Well, too bad. I promised I wouldn't tell anyone who killed my dad and I'm keeping that promise. I'm in the interrogation room when they send a woman in to talk to me. She's the District Attorney. So what, I'm not scared of the DA, woman or not. She's putting a document on the table in front of me. She says it's my father's birth certificate. The name on it is what the killer called Dad, Anthony, so I guess it must be real. I thought his name was Frank. The next piece of information is a surprise. My dad had been a cop. But it is no surprise to hear he had been a dirty cop. Next she hands me a wedding certificate. It has my dad's real name on it. So what? I knew my parents had been married. Wait a minute. The wife's name on the marriage certificate is the same as the woman sitting across from me. My mother is the District Attorney? My dad a crooked cop I can believe. My mother still alive and the District Attorney, now that I am having some trouble accepting. Whatever the case, I am still not telling them who killed my dad. No matter what else this woman tells me.

Excerpt: Page 15 through page 19.

Curriculum Connections: History, Psychology, Sociology

Jude is tried as an adult, even though he is only 15. Schedule time in the library media center for students to research the history of teens being tried as adults and discuss whether they agree with the convictions.

Similar Titles:

Dumas, Alexandre, *The Count of Monte Cristo.* Penguin, 2005, 509pp. $6.95. ISBN: 0451529707. Tander Media, 2006, $99.99. CD. ISBN: 140013210X.

McNally, John, *Troublemakers.* University of Iowa Press, 2000, 224pp. $15. ISBN: 0877457271.

Myers, Walter Dean, *Monster.* Amistad, 1999, 288pp. $15.95. ISBN: 0060280778. Amistad, 2001, 288pp. $7.99. ISBN: 0064407314. Listening Library, 2000, $20. ISBN: 080728257X.

Smith, Roger, *Youth in Prison.* Mason Crest, 2006, 112pp. $22.95. ISBN: 1590849906.

Williams, Stanley Tookie, *Life in Prison.* Seastar, 2001, 80pp. $5.95. ISBN: 1587170949.

58 Myracle, Lauren, *Rhymes with Witches.*

Abrams, 2005, 209pp. $16.95. ISBN: 0810958597. Abrams, 2006, 272pp. $6.95. ISBN: 0810992159.

Web Site: <www.laurenmyracle.com>
Subjects: Body Image, Bullying, Emotional Problems, Friendship, High Schools, Jealousy, Magic, Peer Pressure, Self-Esteem, Teachers, Theft, Witchcraft
Genres: Fantasy, Horror, Supernatural
Levels: BL 8-11, PW 9 up, SLJ 9 up, V 7-12

Annotation: Jane, a geeky new freshman, is offered the open spot in the most popular clique in school, the Bitches, and discovers that witchcraft is what makes them popular, by stealing bits of popularity from other students.

Booktalk: Every high school has the clique of girls that some want to be like and no one wants to cross. In this case the girls are literally called "the Bitches." The Bitches have been part of Crestview High for as long anyone can remember. Did you ever wonder how a clique gets to be the center of attention? What is so special about them? Is it the way they dress? Or what they drive? Jane wonders the same thing and, while her best friend Alicia wants desperately to be a cheerleader, Jane dreams of popularity. What Jane doesn't know is that the Bitches' popularity is offered to the least popular girl in the ninth grade, her, and to keep it Jane has to steal something. Would Jane have jumped at becoming a Bitch and gone through the initiation rites if she knew? Or was she so enamored with being popular that she ignored the obvious? It comes at a cost. After taking the easy way out and stealing from her already unpopular friend Alicia, Jane learns to choose wisely who she steals from as some of the girls can afford to lose a little popularity. Alicia can't. How far would you go to be popular?

Excerpt: Second break on page 12 through page 15.

Curriculum Connections: Psychology, Sociology
Schedule time in the library media center for students to browse through old school yearbooks. Based on what they learned from viewing the photographs and the clubs listed, have students discuss if the focus of the school's popular groups has changed and what societal elements may have influenced the changes.

Similar Titles:
Myracle, Lauren, *ttyl.* Abrams, 2004, 224pp. $15.95. ISBN: 0810948214. Abrams, 2005, 234pp. $6.95. ISBN: 0810987880.
Noel, Alyson, *Art Geeks and Prom Queens.* St. Martin's Press, 2005, 240pp. $8.95. ISBN: 0312336365.
Roberts, Laura Peyton, *The Queen of Second Place.* Random House, 2005, 336pp. $15.95. ISBN: 0385731620. Bantam Doubleday Dell, 2006, 336pp. $5.99. ISBN: 0440238714.
Stolarz, Laurie, *Bleed.* Hyperion, 2006, 240pp. $15.99. ISBN: 078683854X.
Walde, Christine, *The Candy Darlings.* Houghton Mifflin, 2006, 320pp. $8.99. ISBN: 0618589694.

Oates, Joyce Carol, *Freaky Green Eyes.*

59

HarperCollins, 2003, 352pp. $17.89. ISBN: 0066237572. HarperCollins, 2005, 368pp. $6.99. ISBN: 0064473481. Recorded Books, 2004, $45.75. ISBN: 1402584539.

Subjects: Body Image, Crime, Death, Emotional Problems, Family Problems, Fathers and Sons, Journals, Journeys, Mothers and Daughters, Murder, Self-Esteem, Sisters, Stepfamilies, Stress, Violence, Writing
Genres: Mystery, Realistic, Suspense
Levels: BL 7-10, PW 9 up, SLJ 7-10, V 7-9

Annotation: Fifteen-year-old Franky, distraught over her parents' separation and her stepfather's behavior toward her mother, has to find her inner strength when she realizes her father is responsible for her mother's disappearance and death.

Booktalk: I'm Francesca Pierson, but most people call me Franky. What they don't know is that I renamed myself on my 14th birthday. What I should really say is that the guy I had to fight off at a party I wasn't supposed to be at renamed me. When I fought back he said I had freaky green eyes. I don't know where that strong side of me came from but I fought him off and I felt powerful. I *was* Freaky Green Eyes. At the time I thought it was incredible that I had an inner strength I didn't know I possessed. I was pretty quiet at home. I was afraid I might upset my stepfather. He's a high profile sportscaster and his temper is as high profile as his name. Things were getting really tense around the house after Mom moved out. Dad wanted me to hate her. He kept saying she was the one who moved out and left us. She was the horrible woman who deserted her husband and children. But I wondered why she left. Mom wasn't the kind of mother who just left her daughters behind. I watched silently as Dad's temper tantrums and threats against Mom escalated. When Mom disappeared, I knew it was time for Freaky Green Eyes to make an appearance. I can't be silent anymore.

Excerpt: First full paragraph on page 22 through page 25.

Curriculum Connections: Biology, Health, Psychology
When Franky fights off the guy at the party she has amazing strength. Schedule time in the library media center for students to research the effect fear-induced adrenalin has on the body and what a person is able to do physically because of the adrenalin rush.

Similar Titles:
Coman, Carolyn, ***Many Stones.*** Handprint, 2000, 160pp. $15.95. ISBN: 1886910553. Puffin, 2002, 160pp. $5.99. ISBN: 0142301485.
Crutcher, Chris, ***Chinese Handcuffs.*** Greenwillow, 1989, 208pp. $17.99. ISBN: 0688083455. HarperCollins, 2004, 296pp. $6.99. ISBN: 0060598395.
Fitch, Janet, ***White Oleander.*** Little Brown, 1999, 390pp. $24.95. ISBN: 0316569321. Little Brown, 2006, 496pp. $7.99. ISBN: 0316182540.
Lester, Julius, ***When Dad Killed Mom.*** Harcourt, 2001, 192pp. $17. ISBN: 0152163050. Harcourt, 2003, 199pp. $6.95. ISBN: 0152046984.
Oates, Joyce Carol, ***Small Avalanches and Other Stories.*** HarperCollins, 2003, 400pp. $16.99. ISBN: 006001217X. HarperCollins, 2004, 390pp. $7.99. ISBN: 0060012196.

60 Pearson, Mary E., *A Room on Lorelei Street.*

Holt, 2005, 272pp. $16.95. ISBN: 0805076670.

Web Site: <www.marypearson.com/maryepearson_001.htm>
Subjects: Alcoholism, Elderly, Emotional Problems, Mothers and Daughter, Moving, Self-Esteem, Sexual Relationships, Stress
Genres: Realistic
Lists: 2006 BBYA
Levels: BL 9-12, SLJ 10 up

Annotation: Fed up with taking care of her alcoholic mother and working as a waitress to pay the bills, 17-year-old Zoë rents a room on Lorelei Street from the elderly, eccentric Opal Keats, who helps rebuild Zoë's fragile self-esteem.

Booktalk: Zoë (with a f...ing "e" at the end!) has her anger just barely under control. Well, not always under control since she got suspended from class for her outburst about how to pronounce her name. Luckily she can work off some of her anger on the tennis court. But, Zoë has had more than she can handle with being responsible for her alcoholic mother as well as paying for all the household bills. Nevertheless, it take a long time for her to make the decision to move into the room on Lorelei Street, a safe and quiet place in the home of the elderly and eccentric Opal. Opal gives Zoë a delicious touch of caring, something no one in Zoë's family has done for many years. Opal even attends Zoë's tennis matches. The first time Zoë saw Opal there she was so stunned she didn't know how to respond. Life was good on Lorelei Street. But the wonderful feeling of having a safe and calm place to live may be coming to an abrupt end. If Zoë doesn't give her grandmother the registration money for the car she will take it away and Zoë needs the car to get to work. Zoë is frantic to figure out how to come up with rent money after she pays the car registration fee. She will not go crawling back to her mother. That's what her grandmother wants. Zoë does something far from pretty to get the rent money, something that has her walking a thin line between caring if she lives or dies, far away from Lorelei Street. The question is, can she find her way back?

Excerpt: Page 17, from italicized "Home" through page 21.

Curriculum Connections: Career Education, Life Skills, Math
Zoë had to figure out how much money she needed to meet her basic living expenses for a month based on her waitress salary. Schedule time in the library media center for students to examine local newspapers to determine the salary for an average after-school and weekend job as well as the monthly cost for a single room, or as a roommate. Based on what they have learned, have students calculate how many hours a week they would have to work to pay for the rent and buy basic groceries.

Similar Titles:
Koja, Kathe, ***The Blue Mirror.*** Farrar, Straus & Giroux, 2004, 119pp. $16. ISBN: 0374308497. Penguin, 2006, 128pp. $6.99. ISBN: 0142406937.
MacCready, Robin Merrow, ***Buried.*** Penguin, 2006, 224pp. $16.99. ISBN: 0525477241.
Miller, Susan B., ***When Parents Have Problems: A Book for Teens and Older Children with an Abusive, Alcoholic, or Mentally Ill Parent.*** C. Thomas, 1995, 79pp. $23.95. ISBN: 039805990X.
Moore, Peter, ***Blind Sighted.*** Viking, 2002, 272pp. $16.99. ISBN: 0670035432. Puffin, 2002, 204pp. $6.99. ISBN: 0142401269.
Quarles, Heather, ***A Door Near Here.*** Laurel Leaf, 2000, 240pp. $5.50. ISBN: 0440227615.

61 Rapp, Adam, *33 Snowfish.*

Candlewick, 2003, 192pp. $15.99. ISBN: 0763618748. Candlewick, 2006, 179pp. $6.99. ISBN: 0763629170.

Subjects: Child Sexual Abuse, Crime, Death, Drug Abuse, Emotional Problems, Illness, Journeys, Kidnapping, Mental Illness, Murder, Prostitution, Rape, Runaways, Sexual Relationships, Survival, Violence
Genres: Realistic
Lists: 2004 BBYA
Levels: PW 10 up, SLJ 9 up, V 10-12

Annotation: Running from the law in a car Boobie stole after killing his parents and kidnapping his baby brother, the stoic 17-year-old, who speaks via morbid drawings, is joined by Custis, a young boy running from a pedophile, and Curl, a drug addicted teenage prostitute.

Booktalk: There was something about Boobie that drew Custis to him. Custis followed Boobie around for a long time before he ever spoke to him. Boobie, intensely quiet, knew a scruffy boy was following him, but he didn't try to scare him away. It was Boobie's ability to hypnotize people and dogs with his eyes that was really weird. His eyes would go completely black. Custis didn't say a word when he watched an attack dog slink away whimpering after meeting eyes with Boobie. Custis was in even more awe of the older boy than he had been before. Boobie ended up as Custis' best friend by saving his life. Without Boobie, young Custis would still be kept by Bob Motley, a pedophile who used him in homemade horror movies. Boobie took Custis with him when he ran away. Custis went with him willingly even though Boobie came back to their camp site in the woods with his shirt all covered with blood and a baby in his arms. Boobie and Custis are running from the police in Boobie's dead old man's car that they disguised with black spray paint. Boobie brought his girlfriend Curl too. She has the shakes and doesn't like the baby much but she changes his diapers and lets him chew on her fingers when he cries too much. Boobie says they have to get as far away as they can, where no one can find them. Not all of them will survive the journey.

Excerpt: From break on page 21 through page 27.

Curriculum Connections: Art, English
Boobie drew very stark imagines to communicate. Schedule time in the library media center for students to research artistic styles and to choose a style in which to create a self-portrait they think Custis or Curl may have done. To add depth to their visual depiction, have students write an essay to go with their character's self-portrait.

Similar Titles:
Atkins, Catherine, ***When Jeff Comes Home.*** Putnam, 2001, 240pp. $6.99. ISBN: 0698119150.

Cormier, Robert, ***Tenderness.*** Random House, 2004, 229pp. $7.95. ISBN: 0385731337.

Erlbaum, Janice, ***Girlbomb: A Halfway Homeless Memoir.*** Random House, 2006, 272pp. $21.95. ISBN: 1400064228. Villard, 2007, 272pp. $13.95. ISBN: 0812974565.

Johnson, Kathleen Jeffrie, ***Target.*** Roaring Brook, 2003, 192pp. $15.95. ISBN: 0761319328. Random House, 2005, 192pp. $6.50. ISBN: 0440239109.

Rapp, Adam, ***Little Chicago.*** Boyds Mills, 1998, 255pp. $16.95. ISBN: 1886910723.

Reisz, Kristopher, *Tripping to Somewhere.*

62

Simon Pulse, 2006, 368pp. $6.99. ISBN: 1416940006.

Web Site: <www.kristopherreisz.com>

Subjects: Body Image, Cities, Cults, Drug Abuse, Family Problems, Fathers and Daughters, Friendship, Homosexuality, Jealousy, Magic, Music, Runaways, Self-Esteem, Sexual Relationships, Theft, Time Travel, Witchcraft

Genres: Fantasy, Horror, Supernatural

Levels: KL 9–12, PW 9 up

Annotation: Wild girl Sam and her lesbian best friend Gilly chase the centuries' old group of hedonists called the Witches' Carnival, lead by Christopher Marlowe, as they party their way around the world, seeking to join them. Gilly stole $50,000 from her father, a dishonest police officer, so he and his partner are trying to locate them before another police officer does.

Booktalk: I loved her from the moment she slammed into Ashley. I am not a fighter and just continued to put up with Ashley's taunting and teasing me about being a lesbian. I wasn't going to deny it, but I wasn't going to fight back either. Sam body slammed into Ashley on purpose and wasn't about to apologize for it. Sam told Ashley she was my friend and from then on Sam took care of the fighting for me. We were inseparable. My parents weren't too keen on our friendship because Sam comes from a rough family and my dad is a cop. But nothing stopped us from spending time together. We were together the night that psycho Meek came into the gas station wanting cigarettes. Sam gave him lip but I just quietly bought him the cigarettes he wanted. When Sam smart mouthed him and asked if he was going to read my palm to pay for the cigs he did something really gross that I am not sure I can explain. He said he would read the entrails of an animal sacrifice and tore the crow on his shoulder in half, right in front of us. Blood went everywhere. The bird's insides were on the counter and Meek's fingers were in them. Before Sam could chase him out of the gas station he told us that the Witches' Carnival was passing through Atlanta and if we hurried we could catch up with them. He walked away from the gas station with the crow perched on his shoulder, alive and alert. Up until that moment I didn't think anyone believed the Witches' Carnival was real. This group of supernatural travelers was an urban legend, wasn't it? Real or not, the next thing I knew Sam and I were on the road, on our way to Atlanta to join the Witches' Carnival. What a journey it turned out to be. We were *Tripping to Somewhere*.

Excerpt: Page 1 through sixth paragraph on page 6.

Curriculum Connections: English, History

The leader of the Witches' Carnival is supposedly the writer Christopher Marlowe. Schedule time in the library media center for students to research Marlowe to determine and discuss why they think Reisz chose him as the leader of the Witches' Carnival.

Similar Titles:
Duncan, Lois, ***Gallows Hill.*** Laurel Leaf, 1998, 240pp. $5.99. ISBN: 0440227259.
Hyde, Catherine Ryan, ***Becoming Chloe.*** Knopf, 2006, 224pp. $15.95. ISBN: 0375832580.
Maxwell, Katie, ***Circus of the Darned.*** Dorchester, 2006, 182pp. $5.99. ISBN: 0843954000.
Pieczenik, Steve, ***Runaways.*** Tom Clancy's Net Force Series. Berkley, 2001, 192pp. $4.99. ISBN: 0425181502.
Singleton, Linda Joy, ***Witch Ball.*** Seer Series. Llewellyn, 2006, 254pp. $5.99. ISBN: 0738708216.

63 Roth, Matthue, *Never Mind the Goldbergs.*

Scholastic Push, 2005, 360pp. $16.95. ISBN: 0439691885. Scholastic Push, 2006, 368pp. $7.99. ISBN: 0439691893.

Web Site: <www.matthue.com>
Subjects: Acting, Cities, Jewish Americans, Mothers and Daughters, Moving, Music, Occupations, Relationships, Religion, Self-Esteem
Genres: Humor, Multicultural, Realistic
Levels: PW 6 up, SLJ 9 up

Annotation: Seventeen-year-old Hava Aaronson is a New York Orthodox Jew who dresses punk and pushes the boundaries of her religion to the limits when she agrees to act in a TV sitcom about an Orthodox Jewish Family, as the only Jew in the cast.

Booktalk: Hava is just a regular teen in many ways. She has an attitude and an eclectic group of friends. But her life is also based on her Orthodox Jewish values and mandates. Hava loves punk rock, has a colorful vocabulary that is scattered with Yiddish, and spiked hair even more colorful than her vocabulary. She finds it can be more than a little difficult to be in a heavy metal mosh pit and not touch a male in the crowd, but somehow Hava does it. Her exuberance for life has a way of getting Hava in trouble at school and she finds herself in the Rabbi's office more often than she would like. So when Hava gets called down when she is sure she hasn't done anything wrong, she is more than a bit defensive. The Rabbi does indeed have an irritated look on his face, but Hava realizes it has more to do with the phone on his desk than with her. He tells her the phone call is for her and it is a movie producer who has asked for Hava by name. Clearly this interruption at school does not make him happy. Hava is confused. She's acted in a few plays but why is a movie producer calling her at school? Hava learns that he is casting a new television comedy pilot and wants to audition her. Still confused, Hava says she'll have to talk to her parents but her father is in on the conference call. There appears to be no way of getting out of it. As Hava says, "Oy vey, dude!"

Excerpt: Page 1 through page 3.

Curriculum Connections: History, Sociology
Schedule time in the school library media center for students to research what it means to be Orthodox Jewish, and discuss what they learned about the difference between the Jewish religion and the Jewish culture.

Similar Titles:
Kass, Pnina Moed, **Real Time.** Clarion, 2004, 192pp. $15. ISBN: 0618442030. Graphia, 2006, 200pp. $7.99. ISBN: 061869174X.
Pogrebin, Abigail, **Stars of David: Prominent Jews Talk About Being Jewish.** Broadway, 2005, 400pp. $24.95. ISBN: 061869174X.
Roth, Matthue, **Yom Kippur a Go-Go: A Memoir.** Cleis, 2005, 250pp. $14.95. ISBN: 1573442194.
Wex, Michael, **Born to Kvetch: Yiddish Language and Culture in All of Its Moods.** HarperCollins, 2006, 336pp. $13.95. ISBN: 0061132179.
Winston, Hella, **Unchosen: The Hidden Lives of Hasidic Rebels.** Beacon Press, 2005, 224pp. $23.95. ISBN: 0807036269. Beacon Press, 2006, 216pp. $15. ISBN: 0807036277.

64

Schreiber, Ellen, *Vampire Kisses.*

Vampire Kisses Series. HarperCollins, 2003, 197pp. $15.99. ISBN: 006009334X. HarperCollins, 2005, 253pp. $5.99. ISBN: 0060093366.

Web Site: <www.ellenschreiber.com>
Subjects: Bullying, Friendship, High Schools, Peer Pressure, Relationships, Vampires
Genres: Horror
Lists: 2004 QP, 2005 YAC
Levels: BL 7-10, KL 6-12, PW 6 up, SLJ 7 up, V 7-12

Annotation: Sixteen-year-old Goth girl Raven, who has wanted to be a vampire since she was a young child, has fallen for the mysterious new guy in town because she is sure he is a vampire and can make her wishes come true, but he is gone before she can determine who or what he is.

Booktalk: Raven dresses in black and wants be a vampire. This is not a teenage whim. Becoming a vampire was, after all, her career goal in kindergarten. She hasn't changed her mind over the years. She thinks her career goal is attainable when a mysterious family moves into the mansion on the hill. Raven just has to know if they really are vampires as she suspects and breaks into their home. This is when she meets Alexander Sterling, the reclusive homeschooled teenage son, who also dresses all in black. They quickly become a couple and Raven brings him to the Prom, where Travis, her tormenter since they were children, goes after both of them. With a few nasty words he destroys the fragile bonds Raven and Alexander had formed. When Alexander finds out that Raven was initially interested in him only because he might be a vampire, he is devastated and refuses to speak to her. It takes Raven's true friends to throw a dress-in-black party on the Sterling front lawn to get Raven and Alexander back together. Raven is sure her lifelong dream is about to come true, but the house is empty the next day, with no sign of Alexander or his parents, or where they went. What's Raven to do now?

Excerpt: Page 14 to break on page 17.

Curriculum Connections: Geography, History, Sociology
Alexander's family is from Romania, the legendary home of Dracula. Schedule time in the library media center for students to research the history of vampire legends. Have them discuss how the legends vary based on geographical settings.

Similar Titles:
Caine, Rachel, **Glass Houses.** The Morganville Vampires. Penguin, 2005, 256pp. $5.99. ISBN: 0451219945.
Kostova, Elizabeth, **The Historian.** Little Brown, 2005, 656pp. $25.95. ISBN: 0316011770. Little Brown, 2006, 704pp. $15.99. ISBN: 0316154547.
Schreiber, Ellen, **Kissing Coffins.** Vampire Kisses Series. HarperCollins, 2005, 165pp. $15.99. ISBN: 0060776226. HarperTeen, 2007, 240pp. $5.99. ISBN: 0060776242.
Schreiber, Ellen, **Vampireville.** Vampire Kisses Series. HarperCollins, 2006, 192pp. $15.99. ISBN: 0060776250. HarperTeen, 2007, 256pp. $5.99. ISBN: 0060776277.
Smith, L.J., **The Awakening.** Vampire Diaries. HarperCollins, 1999, 311pp. $5.99. ISBN: 0061020001.

Shaw, Tucker, *Flavor of the Week.*

Disney, 2003, 224pp. $15.99. ISBN: 0786818905. Hyperion, 2005, 224pp. $5.99. ISBN: 078685698X.

Subjects: Body Image, Cooking, Friendship, Occupations, Self-Esteem, Weight Control
Genres: Humor, Realistic, Romance
Lists: 2006 PP
Levels: BL 8-10, SLJ 6-9

Annotation: Sixteen-year-old chubby Cyril, whose professional goal is to become a chef, cooks romantic meals for Rose, but he isn't the one on the other side of the table eating them with her because his friend is pretending to have done the cooking. Includes recipes.

Booktalk: Cyril has been baking and cooking for his eccentric parents since he was 12 years old. His career goal is to become a famous chef, but his addiction is Rose Mulligan. At this very moment he is making a batch of her favorite cookies and daydreaming about what he would cook for a private dinner with Rose. She would be so infatuated with both him and the food that she would bring her face in close to his and… His delicious daydream comes to an abrupt end when the oven timer goes off. But a few minutes later he hears Rose's voice in the backyard. Brushing the flour off his jeans, he rushes out to meet her. He doesn't want Rose to know he is the one baking the cookies and certainly not that he is making his special cookies just for her. Cyril isn't embarrassed about his cooking; it's just that talking about cooking is a bit too close to talking about his weight, all 240 pounds of it. Rose is so out of Cyril's league, but that doesn't mean he can't dream. Little does Cyril know that he will soon be cooking the very same romantic dinner for Rose that he has so often daydreamed about, but he won't be the guy across the table from her. Why would Cyril be willing to create a romantic dinner for Rose and another guy?

Excerpt: Page 95 through page 99 (pbk).

Curriculum Connections: Career Education, Life Skills
Cyril wants to be a chef and tries out new recipes regularly. Schedule time in the library media center for students to locate cookbooks and online resources to design a menu for a dinner they would like to cook for someone special.

Similar Titles:
Carle, Megan, ***Teens Cook: How to Cook What You Want to Eat.*** Ten Speed Press, 2004, 146pp. $19.95. ISBN: 1580085849.
McCaughrean, Geraldine, ***Cyrano.*** Harcourt, 2006, 128pp. $16. ISBN: 0152058052.
Shaw, Tucker, ***Everything I Ate: A Year in the Life of My Mouth.*** Chronicle, 2005, 496pp. $14.95. ISBN: 0811847721.
Shaw, Tucker, ***Gentlemen, Start Your Oven: Killer Recipes for Guys.*** Chronicle, 2006, 192pp. $16.95. ISBN: 0811852067.

Whytock, Cherry, *My Cup Runneth Over: The Life of Angelica Cookson Potts.* Simon & Schuster, 2003, 163pp. $14.95. ISBN: 0689865465. Simon & Schuster, 2003, 163pp. $5.99. ISBN: 0689865511.

66 Sleator, William, *The Last Universe.*

Abrams, 2005, 224pp. $16.95. ISBN: 0810958589. Abrams, 2006, 240pp. $6.95. ISBN: 0810992132.

Web Site: <www.cs.cmu.edu/~sleator/billy/index.html>
Subjects: Brothers and Sisters, Disabilities, Emotional Problems, Illness, Jealousy, Time Travel
Genres: Science Fiction
Levels: BL 6-9, PW 6-10, SLJ 6-10

Annotation: Fourteen-year-old Susan and her wheelchair-bound brother, 16-year-old Gary, discover parallel universes that can be entered via the quantum maze in the garden of the old family estate where they are living, even ones where Gary is not ill.

Booktalk: Do you think we will be able time travel in the 21st century? What if we could travel to a parallel time where we still exist but our lives can take a different path? Would you take the chance? That's what happens in this book. When siblings Susan and Gary enter the maze on their family's estate they discover they can enter a parallel world where they still exist but things are not the same. They even meet relatives who they know should be dead. Gary becomes obsessed with visiting the quantum maze and insists Susan push his wheelchair in, even though it scares her. Gary knows something about parallel universes that his sister doesn't. It may be too late for Susan when she realizes, after they come out of the maze, that a change has occurred in their lives. It is a change that could not have happened anywhere but in the maze. Susan knows she should never have listened to Gary. The question is, can she change it back?

Excerpt: Page 27 through page 32.

Curriculum Connections: Biology, Geography, Science
There are species of flowers growing on the family estate that Susan and Gary know are not indigenous to the area. Schedule time in the library media center for students to research a chosen plant species that does not grow in their local area to determine the climactic and soil content reasons why it does not.

Similar Titles:
Chabon, Michael, *Summerland.* Hyperion, 2002, 512pp. $22.95. ISBN: 064156855X. Hyperion, 2004, 500pp. $8.95. ISBN: 0786816155. Highbridge Audio, 2002, $39.95. ISBN: 0641745494. Highbridge Audio, 2002, $39.95. CD. ISBN: 1565117212.

Paul, Richard, ***A Handbook to the Universe: Explorations of Matter, Energy, Space, and Time for Beginning Scientific Thinkers.*** Chicago Review Press, 1993, 308pp. $14.94. ISBN: 1556521723.
Sleator, William, ***House of Stairs.*** Puffin, 1991, 176pp. $5.99. ISBN: 0140345809.
Sleator, William, ***Singularity.*** Puffin, 1995, 176pp. $5.99. ISBN: 0140375988.
Willett, Edward C., ***The Basics of Quantum Physics: Understanding the Photoelectric Effect and Line Spectra.*** Rosen, 2005, 48pp. $25.25. ISBN: 1404203346.

Stratton, Allan, *Chanda's Secrets.* 67

Annick Press, 2004, 196pp. $19.95. ISBN: 1550378351. Annick Press, 2004, 193pp. $8.95. ISBN: 1550378341.

Web Site: <www.allanstratton.com>
Subjects: Africans, Alcoholism, Death, Family Problems, Friendship, Grieving, HIV/AIDS, Illness, Journeys, Medicine, Mothers and Daughters, Prejudices, Prostitution, Stress, Survival
Genres: International, Realistic
Awards: 2005 Printz Honor
Lists: 2005 BBYA, 2005 PP
Levels: BL 9-12, SLJ 8 up

Annotation: Sixteen-year-old Chanda is ashamed of the cruel manner in which her sub-Saharan Africa family and neighbors express their fear of HIV/AIDS when her mother and best friend become ill and fights against the prejudice and ignorance surrounding the need to seek medical care.

Booktalk: I remember when Mama was as big as her belly laugh, but since she married Jonah she has been getting thinner and thinner. She says she needs to put some weight on but Jonah, when he isn't drunk at least, says she is fine the way she is. Jonah makes Mama happy, but I don't understand why. He is always out drinking and cheats on her too. But, at least he doesn't try to do things to me like Isaac did. I am glad Mama found out before Isaac could do anything bad to me, but he threw us out of his house and onto the street. Now we live next to Mrs. Tafa, the worst gossip in the village. Mama tells me that I should just ignore Mrs. Tafa, but the old gossip warned me the other day to stay away from my friend Esther. She suggested that Esther's parents didn't die of cancer and TB as was said at their funerals and that she hoped their sheets were burned. Burned? Why would Esther do that? And, what is Mrs. Tafa talking about when she said her son Emmanuel, who died in a hunting accident, was one of the few who had died pure. What does died pure mean? Getting sick and dying isn't something to be ashamed of, is it?

Excerpt: Page 26 through break on 28.

Curriculum Connections: Health, Sociology

HIV/AIDS in Africa has risen to epidemic proportions. Chanda goes against village taboos and seeks information from the clinic. Schedule time in the library media center for students to research the spread of AIDS/HIV in Africa and why the villagers are afraid to seek assistance.

Similar Titles:

The Children of Africa Confront AIDS: from Vulnerability to Possibility. Ohio University Press, 2003, 296pp. $20. ISBN: 0896802329.

Duggan, Diane, *Out Here by Ourselves: The Stories of Young People Whose Mothers Have AIDS.* Routledge, 2000, 179pp. $125. ISBN: 0815336217.

Greene, Melissa Fay, *There Is No Me without You: One Woman's Odyssey to Rescue Africa's Children.* Bloomsbury, 2006, 480pp. $25.95. ISBN: 1596911166.

Jansen, Hanna, *Over a Thousand Hills I Walk with You.* Carolrhoda, 2006, 342pp. $16.95. ISBN: 1575059274.

Stratton, Allan, *Leslie's Journal.* Annick Press, 2000, 176pp. $19.95. ISBN: 1550376659. Annick Press, 2000, 176pp. $8.95. ISBN: 1550376640.

68 Trueman, Terry, *Cruise Control.*

HarperCollins, 2004, 160pp. $15.99. ISBN: 0066239605. HarperCollins, 2005, 160pp. $6.99. ISBN: 0064473775. Recorded Books, 2005, $31.75. ISBN: 1419331094.

Web Site: <www.terrytrueman.com>
Subjects: Basketball, Brothers, Disabilities, Divorce, Emotional Problems, Fathers and Sons, Friendship, Physically Handicapped, Stress, Violence
Genres: Realistic, Sports
Lists: 2006 SA, 2006 YAC
Levels: BL 7-10, KL 6-12, SLJ 7 up

Annotation: Paul's anger over not being able to attend the college of his choice due to his father leaving and his brother Shawn's cerebral palsy is useful to win games on the basketball court, but out of control on the road.

Booktalk: I'm not like some of those guys you see at school. I *don't* beat up girls. Yeah, yeah, yeah! I have a problem with my temper, but not with girls. My problem is with those smug-faced guys who think they are perfect and that their lives are perfect. Let them live my life for a while. How would you like to be in competition for athletic scholarships and know you can't go away to school because your father deserted his family when we needed him the most. He couldn't handle being around Shawn. Shawn's seizures sent him flying out the door. How does he think the ones he left behind to take care of Shawn are handling the stress? Does he even care? So I am the one who picks Shawn up out of his wheelchair and gets drool all over my shoulder. So what's the big deal that I sometimes lose control and take my anger toward my father out on guys who deserve it, especially that creep who ran the red light in his Camaro and almost ran over a little girl? I left him in the gutter. My buddy Tim says I would have killed him if he hadn't pulled me off. Funny thing is—it wasn't that guy's face I was seeing when I was pounding on him.

Excerpt: From first full paragraph on page 2 through last full paragraph on page 5.

Curriculum Connections: Health, Psychology
Paul fears that their father is contemplating euthanasia because he thinks Shawn is in pain. Schedule time in the library media center for students to research the legal issues surrounding euthanasia and discuss their opinion of its illegality.

Similar Titles:
Deuker, Carl, ***Night Hoops.*** Houghton Mifflin, 2000, 256pp. $15. ISBN: 0395979366. HarperCollins, 2001, 256pp. $6.99. ISBN: 0064472752.
Deuker, Carl, ***Runner.*** Houghton Mifflin, 2005, 224pp. $16. ISBN: 0618542981. Graphia, 2007, 154pp. $7.99. ISBN: 0618735054.
Trueman, Terry, ***Inside Out.*** HarperCollins, 2003, 128pp. $15.99. ISBN: 0066239621. HarperCollins, 2004, 117pp. $6.99. ISBN: 0064473767.
Trueman, Terry, ***No Right Turn.*** HarperCollins, 2006, 176pp. $15.99. ISBN: 0060574917.
Trueman, Terry, ***Stuck in Neutral.*** HarperCollins, 2001, 128pp. $6.99. ISBN: 0064472132.

69

van Diepen, Allison, *Street Pharm.*
Simon Pulse, 2006, 297pp. $6.99. ISBN: 1416911545.
Web Site: <www.allisonvandiepen.com>
Subjects: African Americans, Cities, Crime, Death, Drug Abuse, Fathers and Sons, Gangs, High Schools, Murder, Prison, Relationships, Stress, Violence
Genres: Multicultural, Realistic
Levels: BL 8-11, SLJ 9 up

Annotation: Seventeen-year-old African-American Ty Johnson takes over as drug dealer when his father goes to prison, using his street smarts to keep the business going while attending an alternative high school where he falls for a girl who doesn't know he deals drugs.

Booktalk: I want to tell you about my so called boyfriend Ty. I should have known he was too good to be true. After all, we attend an alternative high school and he does seem a bit too smart and way too well-dressed to be here. I could tell the first day he came to class that he got a bit of an attitude and I liked that about him. I liked him even more when we were paired up to work on assignments. I invited him over to do homework at my place and he was polite to my grandmother and nice to my little boy, even if initially he thought he was my little brother. Because I have a kid is why I'm finishing high school at Les Chancellor Institute of Career Opportunities. If I had been smart I would have asked more questions about why Ty was sent there. I should have known it was more than just him cutting classes. Or at least I should have asked why he got kicked out for cutting so many classes. But by then I was too into him to think straight and I even invited him to my family's annual Halloween party. We don't let the little ones trick or treat in our neighborhood so they trick or treat inside with us. Ty and me, we only went out in public once and he took me all the way to Manhattan that night. Since then we always stay in at my place. I thought it was because he knew I can't afford a babysitter. That ain't it at all. He doesn't want to be seen with me in public and it isn't because he is ashamed of me. Ty is in way over his head and if I am not careful he is going to pull me down with him too. I don't answer his phone calls no more.

Excerpt: Page 16 through page 18.

Curriculum Connections: English, History

Ty is reading *The Art of War* by Sun Tzu, which was written over 2,500 years ago. Schedule time in the library media center for students to research various historical and contemporary references to this ancient classic and how the strategies of war have been used through the ages.

Similar Titles:

Bonham, Frank, ***Durango Street.*** Penguin, 1999, 190pp. $5.99. ISBN: 0141303093.
Hardrick, Jackie, ***Imani in Never Say Goodbye.*** Enlighten Publications, 2004, 272pp. $15. ISBN: 0970622627.
Hill, Ernest, ***Satisfied with Nothin.*** Simon & Schuster, 1997, 320pp. $19.95. ISBN: 0684834057.
Hong, K.L., ***Life Freaks Me Out: And Then I Deal with It.*** Search Institute, 2005, 160pp. $9.95. ISBN: 1574828568.
Lynn, Tracy, ***Rx.*** Simon Pulse, 2005, 272pp. $6.99. ISBN: 1416911553.

70 Vande Velde, Vivian. *The Book of Mordred.*

Houghton Mifflin, 2005, 342pp. $18.00. ISBN: 061850754X. Houghton Mifflin, 2007, 344pp. $8.99. ISBN: 0618809165.

Web Site: <www.vivianvandevelde.com>
Subjects: Fathers and Sons, Friendship, Jealousy, Knights and Knighthood, Magic, Mothers and Daughters, Relationships, Royalty, Violence, War, Witchcraft, Wizards
Genres: Fantasy, Historical, International
Levels: BL 8-11, SLJ 8 up

Annotation: Mordred, a young knight in King Arthur's Court, plays a central role in the lives of a wizard's young widow Alayna, her magically gifted daughter Keira, and Merlin's beloved and manipulative Nimue. Narrated from various perspectives.

Booktalk: Imagine what it must have been like for Mordred, the unwanted son of King Arthur. In most Arthurian legends Mordred is a dark knight and not welcome in Camelot or at his father's table. Instead, think of Mordred as a young knight of the Round Table who is capable of kindness and love. He plays a central role in the lives of three women. First to enter Mordred's life are a magician's widow and her young daughter for whom Mordred takes on the role of guardian. Mordred begins to care deeply for the mother as he looks out for the safety of the daughter who has inherited her father's gift for magic and is used as a pawn by other wizards now that her father is dead. Both mother and daughter love the quiet knight who is their champion. The thorn in their side is Merlin's lover Nimue, who also has a romantic interest in Mordred. Is Nimue really the wicked sorceress who used her magic to lock Merlin inside a tree, or is she his beloved who safely sealed him away as he requested? Only Nimue, and perhaps Merlin, knows the answer to that question, as well as to why she has decided to meddle in Mordred's life. Nimue works her feminine magic on Mordred, working to destroy the fragile family bonds he has formed with the pretty widow and her daughter. Poor Mordred. He doesn't stand a chance against a sorceress.

Excerpt: From sixth paragraph on page 18 through page 22.

Curriculum Connections: English, History

Schedule time in the library media center for students to research the variations in Arthurian legends and other historical documents as to Mordred's role in Camelot and any relationship he may have had to Nimue.

Similar Titles:

Clegg, Douglas, ***Mordred: Bastard Son.*** Alyson Books, 2007, 360pp. $14.95. ISBN: 1555839878.
Miles, Rosalind, ***The Child of the Holy Grail.*** Guenevere Series. Crown, 2002, 512pp. $13.95. ISBN: 0609809563.
Springer, Nancy, ***I Am Mordred: A Tale from Camelot.*** Penguin, 2002, 184pp. $6.99. ISBN: 0698118413.
Stewart, Mary, ***The Wicked Day.*** HarperCollins, 2003, 417pp. $14.95. ISBN: 0060548282.
Thomson, Sarah L., ***The Dragon's Son.*** Orchard, 2001, 181pp. $17.95. ISBN: 0531303330.

71 Whitcomb, Laura, *A Certain Slant of Light.*

Houghton Mifflin, 2006, 288pp. $8.99. ISBN: 0618585328. Listening Library, 2006, $40. ISBN: 073933574X. Listening Library, 2006, $45. CD. ISBN: 073933574X.

Web Site: <www.laurawhitcomb.com>
Subjects: Death, Depression, Drug Abuse, Family Problems, Ghosts, High Schools, Relationships, Religion, Suicide, Teachers
Genres: Supernatural
Lists: 2006 BBYA
Levels: BL 9-12, KL 10 up, PW 9 up, SLJ 9 up, V 10-12

Annotation: Helen, the ghost of a 27-year-old woman who has been dead for 130 years, is haunting an English teacher until she falls in love with another ghost who inhabits the body of a student in the teacher's junior English class. Together, they search for a body for her to inhabit.

Booktalk: I was hovering above Mr. Brown, an English teacher and the latest of the living humans I have haunted in the last 130 years. That's when I saw the boy looking right at me. Living humans are not supposed to see me. I am a ghost. I've been dead for over 130 years so I should know that living humans *cannot* see me. Only other ghosts can. It frightened me that he could actually see me so I slid away and hid but I kept watching him. Whenever he came to class I was in the room, hiding where I could observe him. He always knew I was there. From the outside he looked like so many of the other young people of this time period. He was unkempt with hair hanging in his eyes, but those eyes were very intently watching me. One day my curiosity got the best of me and I waited outside the classroom when he came out. I was hiding behind a tree but he walked right up to it and stopped. He didn't say any thing. He just smiled and began to walk away. I couldn't help myself, I followed him. I could feel myself being pulled in two directions. Normally I would be following the English teacher Mr. Brown, but I had to find out why this boy could see me so I followed him instead. He stopped three feet from the wall behind the school where no one could see him and waited. I surprised myself by marching up to him and demanded to know if he could hear me too. He answered with, "I have ears don't I?" I was so upset by his response that I told him not to speak to me again and I stayed close to Mr. Brown, but my curiosity got the best of me again and I spoke with him. I found out that he too was a spirit, but his spirit had taken over the body of a living boy whose own spirit no longer wanted to be there. The ghost's name was James and we fell in love, but it is difficult to be in love when one of you has a body and the other does not. So now we are looking for a human girl whose spirit is dying inside too. We are looking for a body for me.

Excerpt: First full paragraph on page 104 through third full paragraph on page 108.

Curriculum Connections: English, History
Both James and Helen speak in the more formal English of their day. Schedule time

in the library media center for students to research terms used 150 years ago and compare them to today's slang or terminology.

Similar Titles:
Berry, Liz, *The China Garden.* HarperCollins, 1999, 288pp. $6.99. ISBN: 0380732289.
Blum, Deborah, *Ghost Hunters: William James and the Search for Scientific Proof of Life after Death.* Penguin, 2006, 384pp. $25.95. ISBN: 1594200904.
Cusik, Richie Tankersley, *The House Next Door.* Simon & Schuster, 2002, 272pp. $4.99. ISBN: 0743418387.
Jenkins, A.M., *Beating Heart: A Ghost Story.* HarperCollins, 2006, 256pp. $15.99. ISBN: 0060546077.
McConnell, Kathleen, *Don't Call Them Ghosts: The Spirit Children of Fountaine Manse – A True Story.* Llewellyn, 2004, 264pp. $12.95. ISBN: 0738705330.

72

Wittlinger, Ellen, *Blind Faith.*

Simon & Schuster, 2006, 288pp. $15.95. ISBN: 1416902732.

Web Site: <www.ellenwittlinger.com>
Subjects: Brothers and Sisters, Cancer, Death, Depression, Elderly, Family Problems, Friendship, Grandparents, Grieving, Illness, Mothers and Daughters, Religion, Stress
Genres: Realistic, Religious
Levels: BL 7-10, KL 6-12, PW 6 up, SLJ 7 up, V 7-12

Annotation: When her grandmother Bunny dies, 15-year-old Liz deals with her mother's interest in a spiritualist church, her father's anger over this involvement, and the new neighbors, teenage Nathan and his little sister Courtney, whose mother is dying of leukemia.

Booktalk: When Liz's grandmother Bunny dies, she misses her terribly, but nothing like what is happening to her mother. Liz's mother is desperately grieving as a daughter, a daughter who is incapable of being a mother to her own daughter. Liz is left alone in her grief. Liz wants to believe what she hears at the spiritualist church her mother makes her attend with her every Saturday afternoon. She both loves and hates going with her mother to the readings and truly wants to believe as her mother does. She wants to readily accept the errors in the readings as her mother does, such as the reader seeing a cat in her grandmother's hands but then changing her reading to say it is a baby rabbit. Of course it is a rabbit. Her grandmother's name is Bunny. When Nathan, Courtney, and their dying mother move into old Crabby's house across the street, Liz becomes involved in their lives because of Courtney, who wants a big sister. Whether Liz likes it or not, she has become a central part of Courtney's life since her older brother Nathan is mad all the time and her mother is sick in bed. Courtney needs someone to play with and Liz is too nice not to spend time with her. Liz really likes the little kid—who wouldn't? Courtney is a breath of fresh air. She is a happy person who doesn't know about death yet. Liz certainly wasn't expecting to fall for the angry older brother Nathan, which complicates things in her life even more than her mother's insistence that she is communicating with Bunny.

Excerpt: Beginning with paragraph six on page eight through page 10.

Curriculum Connections: Music, Psychology

Liz loves to play the piano when she is feeling depressed. Mozart is one of her favorite composers. Schedule time in the library media center for students to research composers and their famous pieces, choosing two pieces of music that they think would soothe their soul if they were grieving a loved one.

Similar Titles:

Grollman, Earl A., ***Straight Talk About Death for Teens: How to Cope with Losing Someone You Love.*** Beacon, 1993, 146pp. $14. ISBN: 0807025011.

L'Engle, Madeleine, ***A Ring of Endless Light.*** Farrar, Straus & Giroux, 1980, 324pp. $20. ISBN: 0374362998. Random House, 1981, 336pp. $6.50. ISBN: 0440972329.

Nolan, Han, ***A Face in Every Window.*** Harcourt, 1999, 256pp. $16. ISBN: 0152019154. Penguin, 2001, 264pp. $5.99. ISBN: 0141312181.

Rinaldi, Ann, ***Or Give Me Death: A Novel of Patrick Henry's Family.*** Harcourt, 2003, 240pp. $17. ISBN: 0152166874. Harcourt, 2004, 240pp. $6.95. ISBN: 0152050760.

Wittlinger, Ellen, ***Heart on My Sleeve.*** Simon & Schuster, 2004, 219pp. $16.95. ISBN: 0689033834. Simon Pulse, 2005, 240pp. $6.99. ISBN: 0689849990.

73 Zeises, Lara M., *Anyone But You.*

Delacorte, 2005, 256pp. $15.95. ISBN: 0385731450.

Web Site: <www.zeisgeist.com>
Subjects: Body Image, Brothers and Sisters, Family Problems, Friendship, Jealousy, Relationships, Sexuality, Skateboarding
Genres: Realistic
Levels: BL 10-12, KL 6-12, PW 9 up, SLJ 9 up

Annotation: Fifteen-year-old Seattle and 17-year-old Critter have been pseudo siblings and best friends since their parents got together when they were little kids, but now that they are teens, and attracted to each other, they must redefine their relationship. Written in alternating voices.

Booktalk: Have you ever kept a secret? Most of us have and they usually cause problems, don't they? What if the secret you are keeping is from yourself and it's a secret about your feelings toward someone else? But then again, can it really be a secret if you haven't accepted the fact that what you are feeling is real? Maybe being in denial is a better word for what I am doing rather than keeping a secret. I don't want to deal with what is going on between me and Critter. I am not even sure what *is* going on, but there is something going on between us that I really don't like. All I know is that whatever it is it's making me mad. Every day I get a little more upset with Critter, the very person I have spent most of my waking hours with since I was a little kid. Right now I want to just slug him. Or maybe I'm mad because what I really want to do is to hug him and that idea is too scary for words. Anyway, how dare he get all gooey eyed over some preppie chick? I mean, really. She drives a BMW with leather seats. We ride around town in a car that is so old it has an eight-track player. Deep down inside I know it's partially my fault. I'm the one who convinced Critter to flirt with her, the female lifeguard at the rich kids' pool, so we could get in to cool off. But it was supposed to be a game. He wasn't supposed to really fall for her. And why does Critter think that some rich girl, who by the way has a college-age boyfriend, is going to fall for him, a skinny dweeb who idolizes Rod Stewart? I can't figure out why I am so mad. It isn't like I should be jealous. I have considered Critter my brother for years. So what's the big deal? Why am I so upset with him about this girl?

Excerpt: Page 25 to break on page 32.

Curriculum Connections: Physical Education
Seattle loves to skateboard, a male-dominated sport. Schedule time in the school library media center for students to research a sport that was once dominated by males but has proved to be one that females excel at, such as snowboarding and skateboarding.

Similar Titles:
Brian, Kate, *Megan Meade's Guide to the McGowan Boys.* Simon & Schuster, 2005, 266pp. $15.99. ISBN: 1416900306.
Douglas, Lola, *More Confessions of a Hollywood Starlet.* Razorbill, 2006, 224pp. $16.99. ISBN: 1595140514.
Douglas, Lola, *True Confessions of a Hollywood Starlet.* Razorbill, 2005, 272pp. $16.99. ISBN: 1595140352. Razorbill, 2006, 288pp. $6.99. ISBN: 159514093X.
Ritter, John H., *Under the Baseball Moon.* Philomel, 2006, 204pp. $16.99. ISBN: 0399236236.
Zeises, Lara M., *Contents Under Pressure.* Random House, 2004, 256pp. $15.95. ISBN: 0385730470. Random House, 2005, 256pp. $5.99. ISBN: 0440237874.

74 Zeises, Lara M., *Bringing Up the Bones.*

Random House, 2002, 224pp. $12.95. ISBN: 0385730012. Random House, 2002, 213pp. $5.99. ISBN: 044022974X.

Web Site: <www.zeisgeist.com>
Subjects: Accidents, Death, Depression, Friendship, Grieving, Jealousy, Relationships, Sexual Relationships
Genres: Realistic
Levels: BL 10-12, KL 10-12, PW 9 up, SLJ 10 up

Annotation: Eighteen-year-old Bridget is taking a year off before she goes to college to deal with her grief over the accidental death of Benji, the love of her life who wasn't in love with her. A new relationship helps her take the first steps to make it on her own.

Booktalk: I hadn't gotten over the fact that he didn't love me the way I loved him. I didn't have a chance to change his mind before he died. How could Benji leave me like that? Twice! First he left for California, partially to get away from me. But now he truly is gone. I am trying. I really am. I get up. I go to work. I shoot pool with Fitzi. I even go out with Ellie. I am trying to be normal but they won't let me. A snippet of one of our favorite songs comes on and they all stop and watch me to see what I am going to do. My therapist says I just need time. It's been seven months since Benji died. His car was broad sided by an 18-wheeler when the driver had a heart attack. The doctors said Benji didn't suffer, but he is still dead, and I am the one who is suffering. I admit it, I am not dealing with his death very well. I remember our one time together, the night before he left for California when he told me he loved me. But then I received a letter from him saying that he didn't think love can be reduced to an equation. He wrote "Friendship + Attraction ≠ Love." He wanted to go back to being friends. If I could have him back right now I would be willing to try to do just friendship, but could I? I don't know, but I want the chance to try!

Excerpt: From break on page 75 through page 79.

Curriculum Connections: English, Psychology
Bridget is slowly working her way through the grieving process. Schedule time in the library media center for students to research the stages of grief and chose a poem they think would help Bridget work her way through the process.

Similar Titles:

Deaver, Julie Reece, *Say Goodnight, Gracie.* HarperCollins, 1989, 224pp. $6.99. ISBN: 0064470075.
Hurwin, Davida Wills, *The Farther You Run.* Viking, 2003, 217pp. $16.99. ISBN: 0670036277. Penguin, 2005, 217pp. $6.99. ISBN: 014240294X.
Manning, Sarra, *Let's Get Lost.* Penguin, 2006, 352pp. $16.99. ISBN: 0525476660.

Orr, Wendy, ***Peeling the Onion.*** Holiday House, 1997, 166pp. $16.95. ISBN: 082341289X. Random House, 1999, 166pp. $5.50. ISBN: 0440227739.

Rosoff, Meg, ***Just In Case.*** Wendy Lamb Books, 2006, 256pp. $16.95. ISBN: 0385746784.

75

Zusak, Markus, ***Getting the Girl.***

Scholastic, 2003, 261pp. $16.95. ISBN: 0439389496. Scholastic, 2004, 256pp. $6.99. ISBN: 043938950X.

Web Site: <www.markuszusak.com>
Subjects: Brothers, Brothers and Sisters, Family Problems, Jealousy, Relationships, Self-Esteem, Sexual Relationships, Violence, Writing
Genres: International, Poetry, Realistic
Levels: BL 9-12, KL 7-12, SLJ 8 up

Annotation: Cameron has always been the quiet brother who observes and writes while watching his brothers Steve excel on the soccer field and Ruben win in the boxing ring and romance the girls afterward, but Cameron makes the mistake of falling for one of Ruben's conquests, resulting in violent sibling rivalry.

Booktalk: Cameron is an observer who writes about what he sees and feels rather than getting involved in the action himself. That's not always a bad thing. Sometimes really good things come out of sitting back, watching, and waiting. You may have met Cameron and his aggressive older brother Rube in Zusak's first novel *Fighting Ruben Wolfe*. Rube has proven himself top dog in the illegal fighting ring so he has gone on to a different type of conquest. He is now out to score as many girls as he can. Although Cameron certainly doesn't agree with his brother's behavior and is sometimes downright disgusted by it, Cameron doesn't outwardly react to his older brother's callous treatment of girls as Rube dumps one every couple of weeks so he can move on to his next conquest. That's just Rube—he's got the looks and he knows it. Cameron doesn't show any real interest in his older brother's sexual exploits until Rube dates Octavia. She isn't Rube's type. Octavia doesn't wear tight clothes or too much makeup. And, she doesn't look right through Cameron as if he doesn't exist, like Rube's other girlfriends had. Cameron likes that a lot, so he just sits back while watching and waiting for Rube to dump her. But Octavia beats Rube to the punch and dumps him first. And then, to everyone's surprise, she opens the door wide for quiet Cameron as, in his own unique way, he sets about *Getting the Girl*.

Excerpt: From last paragraph beginning on page 214 to break on page 221.

Curriculum Connections: Psychology
Schedule time in the library media center for students to research sibling rivalry and discuss whether Rube and Cameron fit the stereotypes.

Similar Titles:
Earls, Nick, *After Summer.* Graphia, 2005, 224pp. $6.99. ISBN: 061845781X.
Lipsyte, Robert, *The Brave.* HarperTrophy, 1993, 208pp. $5.99. ISBN: 0064470792.
Schaap, Jeremy, *Cinderella Man.* Houghton Mifflin, 2006, 336pp. $13.95. ISBN: 0618711902.
Waltman, Kevin, *Nowhere Fast.* Push, 2002, 208pp. $6.99. ISBN: 0439414245.
Zusak, Markus, *Fighting Ruben Wolfe.* Push, 2002, 224pp. $6.99. ISBN: 0439241871.

SECTION 6

Indices

For ease of access, the numbers in the indices refer to the entry number, rather than to a page number.

A. Authors

Adlington, L.J., *The Diary of Pelly D* 1
Aidinoff, Elsie V., *The Garden* 2
Bell, Hilari, *Fall of a Kingdom* 3
Bennett, Holly, *The Bonemender* 4
Bennett, James, *Faith Wish* 5
Black, Holly, *Tithe: A Modern Faerie Tale* 6
Black, Holly, *Valiant: A Modern Tale of Faerie* 7
Blackman, Malorie, *Naughts & Crosses* 8
Block, Francesca Lia, *Wasteland* 9
Bowler, Tim, *Apocalypse* 10
Brashares, Ann, *Sisterhood of the Traveling Pants* 11
Bray, Libba, *A Great and Terrible Beauty* 12
Brooks, Bruce, *Dolores: Seven Stories About Her* 13
Brooks, Kevin, *Candy* 14
Brooks, Kevin, *Lucas: A Story of Love and Hate* 15
Brooks, Kevin, *The Road of the Dead* 16
Brooks, Martha, *True Confessions of a Heartless Girl* 17
Burnham, Niki, *Sticky Fingers* 18
Charlton-Trujillo, e.E., *Feels Like Home* 19

Chotjewitz, David, *Daniel Half Human and the Good Nazi* 20
Cirrone, Dorian, *Dancing in Red Shoes Will Kill You* 21
Cohn, Rachel, *Pop Princess* 22
Constable, Kate, *The Singer of All Songs* 23
Corrigan, Eireann, *Splintering* 24
Coy, John, *Crackback* 25
Crutcher, Chris, *Whale Talk* 26
Dines, Carol, *The Queen's Soprano* 27
Doyle, Malachy, *Georgie* 28
Draper, Sharon M., *Copper Sun* 29
Fiedler, Lisa, *Romeo's Ex: Rosaline's Story* 30
Flinn, Alex, *Diva* 31
Flinn, Alex, *Fade to Black* 32
Frank, E.R., *America* 33
Fredericks, Mariah, *Crunch Time* 34
Gantos, Jack, *The Love Curse of the Rumbaughs* 35
Garden, Nancy, *Endgame* 36
Geras, Adele, *Ithaka* 37
Giles, Gail, *Dead Girls Don't Write Letters* 38
Giles, Gail, *Playing in Traffic* 39
Green, John, *Looking for Alaska* 40
Hartinger, Brent, *The Last Chance Texaco* 41
Hartinger, Brent, *The Order of the Poison Oak* 42
Hautman, Pete, *Invisible* 43
Hearn, Julie, *The Minister's Daughter* 44
Hoffman, Alice, *Green Angel* 45
Hoffman, Alice, *Incantation* 46
Hooper, Mary, *Amy* 47
Hopkins, Ellen, *Burned* 48
Jones, Patrick, *Nailed* 49
Kennen, Ally, *Beast* 50
Klass, David, *Firestorm* 51
Klause, Annette Curtis, *Freaks: Alive on the Inside!* 52
Lawrence, Michael, *A Crack in the Line* 53
Lester, Julius, *Time's Memory* 54
Mac, Carrie, *The Beckoners* 55
Meyer, Stephenie, *Twilight* 56
Morgenroth, Kate, *Jude* 57
Myracle, Lauren, *Rhymes with Witches* 58
Oates, Joyce Carol, *Freaky Green Eyes* 59
Pearson, Mary E., *A Room on Lorelei Street* 60
Rapp, Adam, *33 Snowfish* 61
Reisz, Kristopher, *Tripping to Somewhere* 62
Roth, Matthue, *Never Mind the Goldbergs* 63
Schreiber, Ellen, *Vampire Kisses* 64
Shaw, Tucker, *Flavor of the Week* 65

Sleator, William, *The Last Universe* 66
Stratton, Allan, *Chanda's Secrets* 67
Trueman, Terry, *Cruise Control* 68
van Diepen, Allison, *Street Pharm* 69
Vande Velde, Vivian, *The Book of Mordred* 70
Whitcomb, Laura, *A Certain Slant of Light* 71
Wittlinger, Ellen, *Blind Faith* 72
Zeises, Lara M., *Anyone But You* 73
Zeises, Lara M., *Bringing Up the Bones* 74
Zusak, Markus, *Getting the Girl* 75

B. Authors, Similar Titles

Anderson, Laurie Halse, *Catalyst* 18
Anderson, Laurie Halse, *Speak* 33
Anonymous, *Go Ask Alice* 14
Aronson, Marc, *Witch-Hunts: Mysteries of the Salem Witch Trials* 44
Atkins, Catherine, *When Jeff Comes Home* 61
Atwater-Rhodes, Amelia, *Shattered Mirror* 56
Atwood, Margaret, *Cat's Eye* 55
Azuonye, Chukwuma, *Dogon* 54
Bagdasarian, Adam, *First French Kiss: And Other Traumas* 15
Bagdasarian, Adam, *Forgotten Fire* 8
Bardi, Abby, *The Book of Fred* 5
Bauer, Joan, *Hope Was Here* 13
Bell, Hilari, *Forging the Sword* 3
Bell, Hilari, *Rise of a Hero* 3
Bennett, Holly, *The Bonemender's Oath* 4
Berry, Liz, *The China Garden* 71
Bissinger, H.G., *Friday Night Lights: A Town, a Team, and a Dream* 25
Blackman, Malorie, *Knife Edge* 8
Blanco, Jodee, *Please Stop Laughing at Me* 55
Block, Francesca Lia, *The Hanged Man* 9
Blum, Deborah, *Ghost Hunters: William James and the
 Search for Scientific Proof of Life after Death* 71
Bode, Janet, *Voices of Rape* 18
Bone, Ian, *Sleep Rough Tonight* 39
Bonham, Frank, *Durango Street* 69
Bowler, Tim, *River Boy* 10
Boylan, Clare, *Emma Brown* 12
Bradbury, Ray, *Something Wicked This Way Comes* 35
Brashares, Ann, *Forever in Blue: Fourth Summer of the Sisterhood* 11
Brashares, Ann, *Girls in Pants: Third Summer of the Sisterhood* 11
Brashares, Ann, *The Second Summer of the Sisterhood* 11
Bray, Libba, *Rebel Angels* 12

Brian, Kate, *Megan Meade's Guide to the McGowan Boys* 73
Brooks, Kevin, *Martyn Pig* 14
Buckley, Veronica, *Christina, Queen of Sweden:
　The Restless Life of a European Eccentric* 27
Bull, Emma, *Finder: A Novel of the Borderlands* 7
Bull, Emma, *War for the Oaks* 6
Bunn, Ivan, *A Trial of Witches* 44
Bunson, Matthew, *The Vampire Encyclopedia* 56
Burgess, Melvin, *Smack* 33
Butler, Octavia E., *The Parable of the Sower* 45
Caine, Rachel, *Glass Houses* 64
Cappo, Nan Willard, *Cheating Lessons* 34
Card, Orson Scott, *Ender's Shadow* 1
Carle, Megan, *Teens Cook: How to Cook What You Want to Eat* 65
Carter, William Lee, *It Happened to Me: A Teen's Guide to
　Overcoming Sexual Abuse* 33
Cartlidge, Cherese, *Life of a Nazi Soldier* 20
Chabon, Michael, *Summerland* 66
Chbosky, Stephen, *The Perks of Being a Wallflower* 33
Cheripko, Jan, *Sun Moon Stars Rain* 16
Chevalier, Tracy, *The Girl with a Pearl Earring* 2
Clegg, Douglas, *Mordred: Bastard Son* 70
Cochran, Thomas, *Roughnecks* 25
Cohn, Rachel and David Levithan, *Nick and Norah's Infinite Playlist* 49
Cole, Brock, *The Goats* 15
Coman, Carolyn, *Bee and Jacky* 9
Coman, Carolyn, *Many Stones* 59
Connelly, Neil, *St. Michael's Scales* 28
Constable, Kate, *The Tenth Power* 23
Constable, Kate, *The Waterless Sea* 23
Conway, Celeste, *The Melting Season* 31
Cooney, Caroline B., *Goddess of Yesterday* 37
Cooney, Caroline B., *Wanted!* 10
Cormier, Robert, *The Chocolate War* 49
Cormier, Robert, *Heroes* 16
Cormier, Robert, *Tenderness* 61
Corrigan, Eireann, *You Remind Me of You* 24
Cray, Jordan, *Gemini 7. Danger.com* 47
Creech, Sharon, *The Wanderer* 13
Crew, Linda, *The Brides of Eden: A True Story Imagined* 5
Crutcher, Chris, *Chinese Handcuffs* 59
Crutcher, Chris, *Staying Fat for Sarah Byrnes* 42
Crutcher, Chris, *Ironman* 26
Crutcher, Chris, *Stotan* 26
Cusik, Richie Tankersley, *The House Next Door* 71
de la Pena, Matt, *Ball Don't Lie* 50

de Lint, Charles, *The Blue Girl* 6
de Lint, Charles, *Waifs and Strays* 7
Deagan, Kathleen A., *Fort Mose: Colonial America's Black
    Fortress of Freedom* 29
Dean, Carolee, *Comfort* 19
Deaver, Julie Reece, *Say Goodnight, Gracie* 74
Dessen, Sarah, *Just Listen* 11
Dessen, Sarah, *Someone Like You* 17
Deuker, Carl, *Night Hoops* 68
Deuker, Carl, *Runner* 68
Diamant, Anita, *The Red Tent* 2
Dickinson, Peter, *The Tears of the Salamander* 27
Doherty, Berlie, *Holly Starcross* 47
Dokey, Cameron, *The Storyteller's Daughter* 3
Douglas, Lola, *More Confessions of a Hollywood Starlet* 73
Douglas, Lola, *True Confessions of a Hollywood Starlet* 73
Dowd, Olympia, *A Young Dancer's Apprenticeship* 21
Draper, Sharon M., *The Battle of Jericho* 39
Draper, Sharon M., *Forged by Fire* 19
Draper, Sharon M., *Romiette and Julio* 30
Duggan, Diane, *Out Here by Ourselves: The Stories of
    Young People Whose Mothers Have AIDS* 67
Dumas, Alexandre, *The Count of Monte Cristo* 57
Duncan, Lois, *Gallows Hill* 62
Duncan, Lois, *The Third Eye* 10
Dvorson, Alexa, *The Hitler Youth: Marching Toward Madness* 20
Earls, Nick, *After Summer* 75
Engdahl, Sylvia, *Enchantress from the Stars* 1
Engdahl, Sylvia, *The Far Side of Evil* 1
Erlbaum, Janice, *Girlbomb: A Halfway Homeless Memoir* 61
Farmer, Nancy, *The Sea of Trolls* 7
Fiedler, Lisa, *Dating Hamlet: Ophelia's Story* 30
Fitch, Janet, *White Oleander* 59
Fleischman, Paul, *Breakout* 50
Fleischman, Paul, *Whirligig* 52
Flinn, Alex, *Breathing Underwater* 31
Flinn, Alex, *Nothing to Lose* 32
Forde, Catherine, *Fat Boy Swim* 26
Frank, E.R., *Life Is Funny* 8
Frank, E.R., *Wrecked* 33
Fredericks, Mariah, *The True Meaning of Cleavage* 34
Freymann-Weyr, Garret, *The Kings Are Already Here* 21
Frost, Helen, *Keesha's House* 41
Gantos, Jack, *Hole In My Life* 35
Garlock, Michael, *Killer 'Gators and Crocs:
    Gruesome Encounters from Across the Globe* 50

Geras, Adele, *Troy* 37
Gibbons, Kaye, *The Life All Around Me by Ellen Foster* 41
Gideon, Melanie, *Pucker* 42
Giles, Gail, *Shattering Glass* 39
Glass, Linzi, *The Year the Gypsies Came* 16
Glover, Linda K., *Defying Ocean's End: An Agenda for Action* 51
Going, K.L., *Fat Kid Rules the World* 14
Goodman, Alison, *Singing the Dogstar Blues* 53
Gordon, Noah, *The Last Jew* 46
Gore, Al, *An Inconvenient Truth: The Crisis of Global Warming* 51
Green, John, *An Abundance of Katherines* 40
Greene, Melissa Fay, *There Is No Me without You:
   One Woman's Odyssey to Rescue Africa's Children* 67
Gregory, Philippa, *The Queen's Fool* 46
Grollman, Earl A., *Straight Talk About Death for Teens:
   How to Cope with Losing Someone You Love* 72
Haddix, Margaret Peterson, *Leaving Fishers* 5
Halliday, John, *Shooting Monarchs* 28
Hanley, Victoria, *The Seer and the Sword* 4
Hardrick, Jackie, *Imani in Never Say Goodbye* 69
Hartinger, Brent, *Geography Club* 42
Hartinger, Brent, *Grand and Humble* 42
Hartzman, Marc, *American Sideshow: An Encyclopedia of
   History's Most Wondrous and Curiously Strange Performers* 52
Hautman, Pete, *Godless* 2
Hautman, Pete, *Mr. Was* 43
Hautman, Pete, *Rash* 40
Heinlein, Robert, A., *A Door into Summer* 53
Hemphill, Stephanie, *Things Left Unsaid: A Novel in Poems* 24
Herrick, Steven, *The Simple Gift* 24
Hewett, Lorri, *Dancer: Everyone Has a Dream* 21
Hill, Ernest, *Satisfied with Nothin* 69
Hinton, S.E., *The Outsiders* 19
Hobbs, Valerie, *How Far Would You Have Gotten If I Hadn't Called You Back?* .. 48
Hoffman, Alice, *The Foretelling* 45
Hoffman, Mary, *Stravaganza: City of Masks* 27
Hong, K.L., *Life Freaks Me Out: And Then I Deal with It* 69
Hooper, Mary, *The Remarkable Life and Times of Eliza Rose* 27
Hopkins, Ellen, *Crank* 48
Hopkins, Ellen, *Impulse* 48
Howard-Barr, Elissa, *The Truth About Sexual Behavior
   and Unplanned Pregnancy* 17
Hrdlitschka, Shelley, *Dancing Naked* 17
Hughes, Dean, *Soldier Boys* 48
Hurwin, Davida Wills, *Circle the Soul Softly* 9
Hurwin, Davida Wills, *The Farther You Run* 74

Hyde, Catherine Ryan, *Becoming Chloe* 62
Hyde, Margaret O., *Safe Sex 101: An Overview for Teens* 32
Jacobs, Harriet, *Incidents in the Life of a Slave Girl* 29
Jansen, Hanna, *Over a Thousand Hills I Walk with You* 67
Jenkins, A.M., *Beating Heart: A Ghost Story* 71
Jenkins, A.M., *Out of Order* 39
Johnson, Kathleen Jeffrie, *A Fast and Brutal Wing* 43
Johnson, Kathleen Jeffrie, *Target* 61
Jones, Patrick, *Chasing Tail Lights* 49
Jones, Patrick, *Things Change* 49
Jordan, Sherryl, *The Raging Quiet* 44
Jordan, Sherryl, *Secret Sacrament* 4
Kass, Pnina Moed, *Real Time* 63
Kater, Michael H., *Hitler Youth* 20
Kerr, M.E., *Night Kites* 32
Kevles, Daniel, *In the Name of Eugenics: Genetics and
   the Uses of Human Heredity* 35
Klass, David, *California Blue* 51
Klass, David, *Dark Angel* 39
Klause, Annette Curtis, *Blood and Chocolate* 52
Klause, Annette Curtis, *The Silver Kiss* 56
Klein, Lisa, *Ophelia* 30
Knowles, John, *A Separate Peace* 40
Koertge, Ron, *Stoner and Spaz* 15
Koja, Kathe, *The Blue Mirror* 60
Koja, Kathe, *Buddha Boy* 36
Koja, Kathe, *Going Under* 38
Kostova, Elizabeth, *The Historian* 64
Krebs, Betsy, *Beyond the Foster Care System: The Future for Teens* ... 41
Landau, Elaine, *Date Violence* 18
Lasky, Kathryn, *Blood Secret* 46
Laughlin, Terry, *Total Immersion: A Revolutionary Way
   to Swim Better and Faster* 26
Lawrence, Iain, *Ghost Boy* 52
Lawrence, Iain, *The Lightkeeper's Daughter* 15
Lawrence, Michael, *Small Eternities* 53
Lawrence, Michael, *The Underwood See* 53
Layne, Steven L., *This Side of Paradise* 1
Le Guin, Ursula, *The Tombs of Atuan* 23
L'Engle, Madeleine, *Many Waters* 10
L'Engle, Madeleine, *A Ring of Endless Light* 72
L'Engle, Madeleine, *Small Rain* 31
Lester, Julius, *This Strange New Feeling: Three Love Stories from Black History* ... 54
Lester, Julius, *When Dad Killed Mom* 59
Levithan, David, *Are We There Yet?* 9

Lewis, Edward, *Hostile Ground: Defusing and
  Restraining Violent Behavior and Physical Assaults* 24
Lewis, Richard, *The Flame Tree* 5
Lipsyte, Robert, *The Brave* 75
Lockhart, E., *The Boyfriend List: 15 Guys, 11 Shrink Appointments,
  4 Ceramic Frogs, and Me, Ruby Oliver* 11
Lowry, Brigid, *Follow the Blue* 19
Lynch, Chris, *Inexcusable* 18
Lynn, Tracy, *Rx* 69
Lynn, Tracy, *Snow* 6
Mac, Carrie, *Crush* 55
MacCready, Robin Merrow, *Buried* 60
MacDonald, Joan Vos, *Cybersafety: Surfing Safely Online* 47
Mackler, Carolyn, *The Earth, My Butt, and Other Big Round Things* 21
Manning, Sarra, *Guitar Girl* 22
Manning, Sarra, *Let's Get Lost* 74
Marcovitz, Hal, *PCP* 24
Marcovitz, Hal, *Teens and Cheating* 34
Martel, Yann, *Life of Pi* 50
Maxwell, Katie, *Circus of the Darned* 62
Mayer, Melody, *The Nannies* 22
Mayfield, Sue, *Drowning Anna* 55
McCafferty, Kate, *Testimony of an Irish Slave Girl* 29
McCaughrean, Geraldine, *Cyrano* 65
McConnell, Kathleen, *Don't Call Them Ghosts:
  The Spirit Children of Fountaine Manse – A True Story* 71
McCormick, Patricia, *Cut* 28
McDevitt, Jack, *Eternity Road* 45
McGhee, Alison, *Shadow Baby* 12
McLaren, Clemence, *Inside the Walls of Troy* 37
McLaren, Clemence, *Waiting for Odysseus* 37
McNally, John, *Troublemakers* 57
Meyer, Carolyn, *Loving Will Shakespeare* 30
Meyer, Stephenie, *New Moon* 56
Miles, Rosalind, *The Child of the Holy Grail* 70
Miller, Susan B., *When Parents Have Problems: A Book for Teens and
  Older Children with an Abusive, Alcoholic, or Mentally Ill Parent* 60
Minchin, Adele, *The Beat Goes On* 32
Moore, Christopher, *Lamb: the Gospel According to Biff, Christ's Childhood Pal* 2
Moore, Peter, *Blind Sighted* 60
Mosley, Walter, *47* 54
Myers, Walter Dean, *Autobiography of My Dead Brother* 9
Myers, Walter Dean, *Monster* 57
Myers, Walter Dean, *Shooter* 36
Myracle, Lauren, *ttyl* 58
Na, An, *A Step from Heaven* 48

Napoli, Donna Jo, *Beast* 3
Napoli, Donna Jo, *The Magic Circle* 44
Naylor, Phyllis Reynolds, *Including Alice* 13
Nelson, Blake, *The New Rules of High School* 40
Niane, D.T., *Sundiata: An Epic of Old Mali* 54
Noel, Alyson, *Art Geeks and Prom Queens* 58
Nolan, Han, *Born Blue* 31
Nolan, Han, *A Face in Every Window* 72
Nolan, Han, *If I Should Die Before I Wake* 1
Oates, Joyce Carol, *After the Wreck, I Picked Myself Up,
   Spread My Wings, and Flew Away* 38
Oates, Joyce Carol, *Sexy* 26
Oates, Joyce Carol, *Small Avalanches and Other Stories* 59
Olin, Sean, *Killing Britney* 36
Orr, Wendy, *Peeling the Onion* 74
Paris, Erna, *The End of Days: A Story of Tolerance,
   Tyranny and the Expulsion of Jews from Spain* 46
Patterson, James, *Maximum Ride: The Angel Experiment* 51
Paul, Richard, *A Handbook to the Universe: Explorations of Matter,
   Energy, Space, and Time for Beginning Scientific Thinkers* 66
Pearson, Mary E., *Scribbler of Dreams* 16
Peck, Richard, *The Last Safe Place on Earth* 5
Pennebaker, Ruth, *Don't Think Twice* 17
Picoult, Jodi, *My Sister's Keeper* 38
Pieczenik, Steve, *Runaways* 62
Pierce, Tamora, *Trickster's Choice* 23
Plum-Ucci, Carol, *What Happened to Lani Garner?* 15
Pollack, Jenny, *Klepto* 18
Powell, Randy, *Three Clams and an Oyster* 25
Power, Ashley, *Goosehead Guide to Life* 47
Pogrebin, Abigail, *Stars of David: Prominent Jews Talk About Being Jewish* 63
Prose, Francine, *After* 36
Pullman, Philip, *The Golden Compass* 23
Qualey, Marsha, *One Night* 14
Quarles, Heather, *A Door Near Here* 60
Rapp, Adam, *The Buffalo Tree* 41
Rapp, Adam, *Little Chicago* 61
Rapp, Adam, *Under the Wolf, Under the Dog* 14
Rees, Celia, *Sorceress* 8
Rice, David Talbot, *Crazy Loco* 19
Rinaldi, Ann, *A Break with Charity: A Story About the Salem Witch Trials* 44
Rinaldi, Ann, *Hang a Thousand Trees with Ribbons* 29
Rinaldi, Ann, *Or Give Me Death: A Novel of Patrick Henry's Family* 72
Rinaldi, Robin, *Ballet* 21
Ritter, John H., *Under the Baseball Moon* 73
Roberts, Laura Peyton, *The Queen of Second Place* 58

Rosoff, Meg, *How I Live Now* .45
Rosoff, Meg, *Just In Case* .74
Roth, Matthue, *Yom Kippur a Go-Go: A Memoir* .63
Rottman, S.L., *Rough Waters* .50
Rottman, S.L., *Shadow of a Doubt* .16
Sanchez, Alex, *Rainbow High* .42
Schaap, Jeremy, *Cinderella Man* .75
Schiller, Lori, *The Quiet Room: A Journey Out of the Torment of Madness* .43
Schreiber, Ellen, *Kissing Coffins* .64
Schreiber, Ellen, *Vampireville* .64
Schutz, Samantha, *I Don't Want to Be Crazy* .38
Shaw, Tucker, *Confessions of a Backup Dancer* .22
Shaw, Tucker, *Everything I Ate: A Year in the Life of My Mouth* .65
Shaw, Tucker, *Gentlemen, Start Your Oven: Killer Recipes for Guys* .65
Shetterly, Will, *Elsewhere* .7
Shetterly, Will, *Nevernever* .6
Siegel, Deborah Spector, *Cross by Day, the Mezzuzah by Night* .46
Simmons, Rachel, *Odd Girl Speaks Out: Girls Write About Bullies, Cliques, Popularity, and Jealousy* .55
Simon, H.W., *100 Great Operas and Their Stories* .31
Singleton, Linda Joy, *Witch Ball* .62
Sleator, William, *House of Stairs* .66
Sleator, William, *Singularity* .66
Smith, L.J., *The Awakening* .64
Smith, Roger, *Youth in Prison* .57
Smith, Sherwood, *Crown Duel* .4
Sorrells, Walter, *Club Dread* .22
Sparks, Beatrice, *Finding Katie: The Diary of Anonymous, a Teenager in Foster Care* .41
Spiegler, Louise, *The Amethyst Road* .7
Spinelli, Jerry, *Milkweed* .20
Spinelli, Jerry, *Stargirl* .13
Spring, Albert, *Steroids and Your Muscles: The Incredible Disgusting Story* .25
Springer, Nancy, *I Am Mordred: A Tale from Camelot* .70
Steele, Julia, *The Taker* .34
Stewart, Mary, *The Wicked Day* .70
Stevermer, Caroline, *A College of Magics* .12
Stolarz, Laurie, *Bleed* .58
Strasser, Todd, *Give a Boy a Gun* .36
Stratton, Allan, *Leslie's Journal* .67
Strong, Susan, *The Boldness of Boys: Famous Men Talk About Growing Up* .52
Sturtevant, Katherine, *A True and Faithful Narrative* .27
Sutcliff, Rosemary, *Black Ships Before Troy: The Story of the Iliad* .37
Tarbox, Katherine, *A Girl's Life Online* .47
Tarnowska, Wafa, *The Seven Wise Princesses: A Medieval Persian Epic* .3
Taylor, Mildred, *The Land* .54

Tharp, Tim, *Knights of the Hill Country* 25
Thomas, Rob, *Rats Saw God* 49
Thomson, Sarah L., *The Dragon's Son* 70
Tolkien, J.R.R., *The Silmarillion* 4
Triana, Gaby, *Backstage Pass* 22
Trueman, Terry, *Inside Out* 68
Trueman, Terry, *No Right Turn* 68
Trueman, Terry, *Stuck in Neutral* 68
Vande Velde, Vivian, *Companions of the Night* 56
Vizzini, Ned, *Be More Chill* 43
Voigt, Cynthia, *Dicey's Song* 13
Walde, Christine, *The Candy Darlings* 58
Waltman, Kevin, *Nowhere Fast* 75
Weaver, Will, *Full Service* 40
Werlin, Nancy, *Double Helix* 35
Westerfeld, Scott, *Blue Noon* 10
Westerfeld, Scott, *The Last Days* 45
Westerfeld, Scott, *The Secret Hour* 53
Wex, Michael, *Born to Kvetch: Yiddish Language
   and Culture in All of Its Moods* 63
Whytock, Cherry, *My Cup Runneth Over: The Life of Angelica Cookson Potts* ...65
Willard, Nancy, *The Tale of Paradise Lost: Based on the Poem by John Milton* 2
Willet, Edward C., *The Basics of Quantum Physics:
   Understanding the Photoelectric Effect and Line Spectra* 66
Williams, Stanley Tookie, *Life in Prison* 57
Winick, Judd, *Pedro and Me: Friendship, Loss and What I Learned* 32
Winston, Hella, *Unchosen: The Hidden Lives of Hasidic Rebels* 63
Wittlinger, Ellen, *Heart on My Sleeve* 72
Wittlinger, Ellen, *The Long Night of Leo and Bree* 38
Woodard, Colin, *Ocean's End: Travels Through Endangered Seas* 51
Woodson, Jacqueline, *The Dear One* 17
Woodson, Jacqueline, *If You Come Softly* 8
Wrede, Patricia C., *Sorcery and Cecelia or the Enchanted Chocolate
   Pot: Being the Correspondence of Two Young Ladies of Quality Regarding
   Various Magical Scandals in London and the Country* 12
Wulffson, Don, *Soldier X* 20
Zeises, Lara M., *Contents Under Pressure* 73
Zephaniah, Benjamin, *Gangsta Rap* 28
Zusak, Markus, *Fighting Ruben Wolfe* 75
Zusak, Markus, *I Am the Messenger* 6

C. Titles

33 Snowfish by Adam Rapp 61

America by E.R. Frank 33
Amy by Mary Hooper 47
Anyone But You by Lara M. Zeises 73
Apocalypse by Tim Bowler 10
Beast by Ally Kennen 50
Beckoners, The by Carrie Mac 55
Blind Faith by Ellen Wittlinger 72
Bonemender, The by Holly Bennett 4
Book of Mordred, The by Vivian Vande Velde 70
Bringing Up the Bones by Lara M. Zeises 74
Burned by Ellen Hopkins 48
Candy by Kevin Brooks 14
Certain Slant of Light, A by Laura Whitcomb 71
Chanda's Secrets by Allan Stratton 67
Copper Sun by Sharon M. Draper 29
Crack in the Line, A by Michael Lawrence 53
Crackback by John Coy 25
Cruise Control by Terry Trueman 68
Crunch Time by Mariah Fredericks 34
Dancing in Red Shoes Will Kill You by Dorian Cirrone 21
Daniel Half Human and the Good Nazi by David Chotjewitz 20
Dead Girls Don't Write Letters by Gail Giles 38
Diary of Pelly D, The by L.J. Adlington 1
Diva by Alex Flinn 31
Dolores: Seven Stories About Her by Bruce Brooks 13
Endgame by Nancy Garden 36
Fade to Black by Alex Flinn 32
Faith Wish by James Bennett 5
Fall of a Kingdom by Hilari Bell 3
Feels Like Home by e.E. Charlton-Trujillo 19
Firestorm by David Klass 51
Flavor of the Week by Tucker Shaw 65
Freaks: Alive on the Inside! by Annette Curtis Klause 52
Freaky Green Eyes by Joyce Carol Oates 59
Garden, The by Elsie V. Aidinoff 2
Georgie by Malachy Doyle 28
Getting the Girl by Markus Zusak 75
Great and Terrible Beauty, A by Libba Bray 12
Green Angel by Alice Hoffman 45
Incantation by Alice Hoffman 46
Invisible by Pete Hautman 43
Ithaka by Adele Geras 37
Jude by Kate Morgenroth 57
Last Chance Texaco, The by Brent Hartinger 41
Last Universe, The by William Sleator 66
Looking for Alaska by John Green 40

Love Curse of the Rumbaughs, The by Jack Gantos 35
Lucas: A Story of Love and Hate by Kevin Brooks 15
Minister's Daughter, The by Julie Hearn 44
Nailed by Patrick Jones 49
Naughts & Crosses by Malorie Blackman 8
Never Mind the Goldbergs by Matthue Roth 63
Order of the Poison Oak, The by Brent Hartinger 42
Playing in Traffic by Gail Giles 39
Pop Princess by Rachel Cohn 22
Queen's Soprano, The by Carol Dines 27
Rhymes with Witches by Lauren Myracle 58
Road of the Dead, The by Kevin Brooks 16
Romeo's Ex: Rosaline's Story by Lisa Fiedler 30
Room on Lorelei Street, A by Mary E. Pearson 60
Singer of All Songs, The by Kate Constable 23
Sisterhood of the Traveling Pants by Ann Brashares 11
Sticky Fingers by Niki Burnham 18
Splintering by Eireann Corrigan 24
Street Pharm by Allison van Diepen 69
Time's Memory by Julius Lester 54
Tithe: A Modern Faerie Tale by Holly Black 6
Tripping to Somewhere by Kristopher Reisz 62
True Confessions of a Heartless Girl by Martha Brooks 17
Twilight by Stephenie Meyer 56
Valiant: A Modern Tale of Faerie by Holly Black 7
Vampire Kisses by Ellen Schreiber 64
Wasteland by Francesca Lia Block 9
Whale Talk by Chris Crutcher 26

D. Titles, Similar

47 by Walter Mosley 54
100 Great Operas and Their Stories by H.W. Simon 31
Abundance of Katherines, An by John Green 40
After by Francine Prose 36
After Summer by Nick Earls 75
*After the Wreck, I Picked Myself Up, Spread My Wings,
   and Flew Away* by Joyce Carol Oates 38
*American Sideshow: An Encyclopedia of History's Most Wondrous
   and Curiously Strange Performers* by Marc Hartzman 52
Amethyst Road, The by Louise Spiegler 7
Are We There Yet? by David Levithan 9
Art Geeks and Prom Queens by Alyson Noel 58
Autobiography of My Dead Brother by Walter Dean Myers 9
Awakening, The by L.J. Smith 64

Backstage Pass by Gaby Triana 22
Ball Don't Lie by Matt de la Pena 50
Ballet by Robin Rinaldi 21
*Basics of Quantum Physics: Understanding the
   Photoelectric Effect and Line Spectra, The* by Edward C. Willett 66
Battle of Jericho, The by Sharon M. Draper 39
Be More Chill by Ned Vizzini 43
Beast by Donna Jo Napoli 3
Beat Goes On, The by Adele Minchin 32
Beating Heart: A Ghost Story by A.M. Jenkins 71
Becoming Chloe by Catherine Ryan Hyde 62
Bee and Jacky by Carolyn Coman 9
Beyond the Foster Care System: The Future for Teens by Betsy Krebs 41
Black Ships Before Troy: The Story of the Iliad by Rosemary Sutcliff 37
Bleed by Laurie Stolarz 58
Blind Sighted by Peter Moore 60
Blood and Chocolate by Annette Curtis Klause 52
Blood Secret by Kathryn Lasky 46
Blue Girl, The by Charles de Lint 6
Blue Mirror, The by Kathe Koja 60
Blue Noon by Scott Westerfeld 10
Boldness of Boys: Famous Men Talk About Growing Up, The by Susan Strong 52
Bonemender's Oath, The by Holly Bennett 4
Book of Fred, The by Abby Bardi 5
Born Blue by Han Nolan 31
*Born to Kvetch: Yiddish Language and Culture in
   All of Its Moods* by Michael Wex 63
*Boyfriend List: 15 Guys, 11 Shrink Appointments, 4 Ceramic Frogs,
   and Me, Ruby Oliver, The* by E. Lockhart 11
Brave, The by Robert Lipsyte 75
Break with Charity: A Story About the Salem Witch Trials, A by Ann Rinaldi ...44
Breakout by Paul Fleischman 50
Breathing Underwater by Alex Flinn 31
Brides of Eden: A True Story Imagined, The by Linda Crew 5
Buddha Boy by Kathe Koja 36
Buffalo Tree, The by Adam Rapp 41
Buried by Robin Merrow MacCready 60
California Blue by David Klass 51
Candy Darlings, The by Christine Walde 58
Catalyst by Laurie Halse Anderson 18
Cat's Eye by Margaret Atwood 55
Chasing Tail Lights by Patrick Jones 49
Cheating Lessons by Nan Willard Cappo 34
Child of the Holy Grail, The by Rosalind Miles 70
Children of Africa Confront AIDS: from Vulnerability to Possibility, The 67
China Garden, The by Liz Berry 71

Chinese Handcuffs by Chris Crutcher 59
Chocolate War, The by Robert Cormier 49
*Christina, Queen of Sweden: The Restless Life of a
   European Eccentric* by Veronica Buckley 27
Cinderella Man by Jeremy Schaap 75
Circle the Soul Softly by Davida Wills Hurwin 9
Circus of the Darned by Katie Maxwell 62
Club Dread by Walter Sorrells 22
College of Magics, A by Caroline Stevermer 12
Comfort by Carolee Dean 19
Companions of the Night by Vivian Vande Velde 56
Confessions of a Backup Dancer by Tucker Shaw 22
Contents Under Pressure by Lara M. Zeises 73
Count of Monte Cristo, The by Alexandre Dumas 57
Crank by Ellen Hopkins 48
Crazy Loco by David Talbot Rice 19
Cross by Day, the Mezzuzah by Night, The by Deborah Spector Siegel .. 46
Crown Duel by Sherwood Smith 4
Crush by Carrie Mac 55
Cut by Patricia McCormick 28
Cybersafety: Surfing Safely Online by Joan Vos MacDonald 47
Cyrano by Geraldine McCaughrean 65
Dancer: Everyone Has a Dream by Lorri Hewett 21
Dancing Naked by Shelley Hrdlitschka 17
Dark Angel by David Klass 39
Date Violence by Elaine Landau 18
Dating Hamlet: Ophelia's Story by Lisa Fiedler 30
Dear One, The by Jacqueline Woodson 17
Defying Ocean's End: An Agenda for Action by Linda K. Glover 51
Dicey's Song by Cynthia Voigt 13
Dogon by Chukwuma Azuonye 54
*Don't Call Them Ghosts: The Spirit Children of
   Fountaine Manse – A True Story* by Kathleen McConnell 71
Don't Think Twice by Ruth Pennebaker 17
Door Into Summer, A by Robert A. Heinlein 53
Door Near Here, A by Heather Quarles 60
Double Helix by Nancy Werlin 35
Dragon's Son, The by Sarah L. Thomson 70
Drowning Anna by Sue Mayfield 55
Durango Street by Frank Bonham 69
Earth, My Butt, and Other Big Round Things, The by Carolyn Mackler 21
Elsewhere by Will Shetterly 7
Emma Brown by Clare Boylan 12
Enchantress from the Stars by Sylvia Engdahl 1
*End of Days: A Story of Tolerance, Tyranny and the
   Expulsion of Jews from Spain, The* by Erna Paris 46

Ender's Shadow by Orson Scott Card 1
Eternity Road by Jack McDevitt 45
Everything I Ate: A Year in the Life of My Mouth by Tucker Shaw 65
Face in Every Window, A by Han Nolan 72
Far Side of Evil, The by Sylvia Engdahl 1
Farther You Run, The by Davida Wills Hurwin 74
Fast and Brutal Wing, A by Kathleen Jeffrie Johnson 43
Fat Boy Swim by Catherine Forde 26
Fat Kid Rules the World by K.L. Going 14
Fighting Ruben Wolfe by Markus Zusak 75
Finder: A Novel of the Borderlands by Emma Bull 7
*Finding Katie: The Diary of Anonymous, a
   Teenager in Foster Care* by Beatrice Sparks 41
First French Kiss: And Other Traumas by Adam Bagdasarian 15
Flame Tree, The by Richard Lewis 5
Follow the Blue by Brigid Lowry 19
Foretelling, The by Alice Hoffman 45
Forever in Blue: Fourth Summer of the Sisterhood by Ann Brashares 11
Forged by Fire by Sharon M. Draper 19
Forging the Sword by Hilari Bell 3
Forgotten Fire by Adam Bagdasarian 8
*Fort Mose: Colonial America's Black Fortress
   of Freedom* by Kathleen A. Deagan 29
Friday Night Lights: A Town, a Team, and a Dream by H.G. Bissinger 25
Full Service by Will Weaver 40
Gallows Hill by Lois Duncan 62
Gangsta Rap by Benjamin Zephaniah 28
Gemini 7. Danger.com by Jordan Cray 47
Gentlemen, Start Your Oven: Killer Recipes for Guys by Tucker Shaw 65
Geography Club by Brent Hartinger 42
Ghost Boy by Iain Lawrence 52
*Ghost Hunters: William James and the Search for Scientific
   Proof of Life after Death* by Deborah Blum 71
Girl with a Pearl Earring, The by Tracy Chevalier 2
Girlbomb: A Halfway Homeless Memoir by Janice Erlbaum 61
Girls in Pants: Third Summer of the Sisterhood by Ann Brashares 11
Girl's Life Online, A by Katherine Tarbox 47
Give a Boy a Gun by Todd Strasser 36
Glass Houses by Rachel Caine 64
Go Ask Alice by Anonymous 14
Goats, The by Brock Cole 15
Goddess of Yesterday by Caroline B. Cooney 37
Godless by Pete Hautman 2
Going Under by Kathe Koja 38
Golden Compass, The by Philip Pullman 23
Goosehead Guide to Life by Ashley Power 47

Gothic!: Ten Original Dark Tales 35
Grand and Humble by Brent Hartinger 42
Growing Up in Slavery: Stories of Young Slaves as Told by Themselves 29
Guitar Girl by Sarra Manning 22
*Handbook to the Universe: Explorations of Matter, Energy, Space,
   and Time for Beginning Scientific Thinkers, A* by Richard Paul 66
Hang a Thousand Trees with Ribbons by Ann Rinaldi 29
Hanged Man, The by Francesca Lia Block 9
Heart on My Sleeve by Ellen Wittlinger 72
Heroes by Robert Cormier 16
Historian, The by Elizabeth Kostova 64
Hitler Youth by Michael H. Kater 20
Hitler Youth: Marching toward Madness, The by Alexa Dvorson 20
Hole In My Life by Jack Gantos 35
Holly Starcross by Berlie Doherty 47
Hope Was Here by Joan Bauer 13
*Hostile Ground: Defusing and Restraining Violent Behavior
   and Physical Assaults* by Edward Lewis 24
House Next Door, The by Richie Tankersley Cusik 71
House of Stairs by William Sleator 66
How Far Would You Have Gotten If I Hadn't Called You Back? by Valerie Hobbs . . .48
How I Live Now by Meg Rosoff 45
I Am Mordred: A Tale from Camelot by Nancy Springer 70
I Am the Messenger by Markus Zusak 6
I Don't Want to Be Crazy by Samantha Schutz 38
I Wrote on All Four Walls: Teens Speak Out on Violence 28
If I Should Die Before I Wake by Han Nolan 1
If You Come Softly by Jacqueline Woodson 8
Imani in Never Say Goodbye by Jackie Hardrick .69
Impulse by Ellen Hopkins 48
*In the Name of Eugenics: Genetics and the
   Uses of Human Heredity* by Daniel Kevles 35
Incidents in the Life of a Slave Girl by Harriet Jacobs 29
Including Alice by Phyllis Reynolds Naylor 13
Inconvenient Truth: The Crisis of Global Warming, An by Al Gore 51
Inexcusable by Chris Lynch 18
Inside Out by Terry Trueman 68
Inside the Walls of Troy by Clemence McLaren 37
Ironman by Chris Crutcher 26
*It Happened to Me: A Teen's Guide to Overcoming
   Sexual Abuse* by William Lee Carter 33
Just In Case by Meg Rosoff 74
Just Listen by Sarah Dessen 11
Keesha's House by Helen Frost 41
Killer 'Gators and Crocs: Gruesome Encounters from

across the Globe by Michael Garlock 50
Killing Britney by Sean Olin 36
Kings Are Already Here, The by Garret Freymann-Weyr 21
Kissing Coffins by Ellen Schreiber 64
Klepto by Jenny Pollack 18
Knife Edge by Malorie Blackman 8
Knights of the Hill Country by Tim Tharp 25
*Lamb: the Gospel According to Biff,
   Christ's Childhood Pal* by Christopher Moore 2
Land, The by Mildred Taylor 54
Last Days, The by Scott Westerfeld 45
Last Jew, The by Noah Gordon 46
Last Safe Place on Earth, The by Richard Peck 5
Leaving Fishers by Margaret Peterson Haddix 5
Leslie's Journal by Allan Stratton 67
Let's Get Lost by Sarra Manning 74
Life All Around Me by Ellen Foster, The by Kaye Gibbons 41
Life Freaks Me Out: And Then I Deal with It by K.L. Hong 69
Life in Prison by Stanley Tookie Williams 57
Life Is Funny by E.R. Frank 8
Life of a Nazi Soldier by Cherese Cartlidge 20
Life of Pi by Yann Martel 50
Lightkeeper's Daughter, The by Iain Lawrence 15
Little Chicago by Adam Rapp 61
Long Night of Leo and Bree, The by Ellen Wittlinger 38
Loving Will Shakespeare by Carolyn Meyer 30
Magic Circle, The by Donna Jo Napoli 44
Manga Shakespeare: Romeo and Juliet 30
Many Stones by Carolyn Coman 59
Many Waters by Madeleine L'Engle 10
Martyn Pig by Kevin Brooks 14
Maximum Ride: The Angel Experiment by James Patterson 51
Megan Meade's Guide to the McGowan Boys by Kate Brian 73
Melting Season, The by Celeste Conway 31
*Mental Health Information for Teens: Health Tips About Mental Wellness
   and Mental Illness: Including Facts About Mental and Emotional Health,
   Depression and Other Mood Disorders, Anxiety Disorders, Behavior
   Disorders, Self-Injury, Psychosis* 43
Milkweed by Jerry Spinelli 20
Monster by Walter Dean Myers 57
Mordred: Bastard Son by Douglas Clegg 70
More Confessions of a Hollywood Starlet by Lola Douglas 73
Mr. Was by Pete Hautman 43
My Cup Runneth Over: The Life of Angelica Cookson Potts by Cherry Whytock 65
My Sister's Keeper by Jodi Picoult 38
Nannies, The by Melody Mayer 22

Nevernever by Will Shetterly 6
New Moon by Stephenie Meyer .... .56
*New Rules of College Admissions: Ten Former Administration
   Officers Reveal What It Takes to Get into College Today, The* .... .34
New Rules of High School, The by Blake Nelson .... .40
Nick and Norah's Infinite Playlist by Rachel Cohn and David Levithan ...... .49
Night Hoops by Carl Deuker .... .68
Night Kites by M.E. Kerr .... .32
No Right Turn by Terry Trueman .... .68
Nothing to Lose by Alex Flinn .... .32
Nowhere Fast by Kevin Waltman .... .75
Ocean's End: Travels Through Endangered Seas by Colin Woodard .... .51
*Odd Girl Speaks Out: Girls Write About Bullies, Cliques,
   Popularity, and Jealousy* by Rachel Simmons .... .55
One Night by Marsha Qualey .... .14
Ophelia by Lisa Klein .... .30
Or Give Me Death: A Novel of Patrick Henry's Family by Ann Rinaldi ...... .72
*Out Here By Ourselves: The Stories of Young People
   Whose Mothers Have AIDS* by Diane Duggan .... .67
Out of Order by A.M. Jenkins .... .39
Outsiders, The by S.E. Hinton .... .19
Over a Thousand Hills I Walk with You by Hanna Jansen .... .67
Parable of the Sower, The by Octavia E. Butler .... .45
PCP by Hal Marcovitz .... .24
Pedro and Me: Friendship, Loss and What I Learned by Judd Winick ...... .32
Peeling the Onion by Wendy Orr .... .74
Perks of Being a Wallflower, The by Stephen Chbosky .... .33
Please Stop Laughing at Me by Jodee Blanco .... .55
Pucker by Melanie Gideon .... .42
Queen of Second Place, The by Laura Peyton Roberts .... .58
Queen's Fool, The by Philippa Gregory .... .46
Quiet Room: A Journey Out of the Torment of Madness, The by Lori Schiller .43
Raging Quiet, The by Sherryl Jordan .... .44
Rainbow High by Alex Sanchez .... .42
Rash by Pete Hautman .... .40
Rats Saw God by Rob Thomas .... .49
Real Time by Pnina Moed Kass .... .63
Rebel Angels by Libba Bray .... .12
Red Tent, The by Anita Diamant 2
Remarkable Life and Times of Eliza Rose, The by Mary Hooper .... .27
Ring of Endless Light, A by Madeleine L'Engle .... .72
Rise of a Hero by Hilari Bell 3
River Boy by Tim Bowler .... .10
Romiette and Julio by Sharon M. Draper .... .30
Rough Waters by S.L. Rottman .... .50
Roughnecks by Thomas Cochran .... .25

Runaways by Steve Pieczenik 62
Runner by Carl Deuker 68
Rx by Tracy Lynn 69
Safe Sex 101: An Overview for Teens by Margaret O. Hyde 32
Satisfied with Nothin by Ernest Hill 69
Say Goodnight, Gracie by Julie Reece Deaver 74
Scribbler of Dreams by Mary E. Pearson 16
Sea of Trolls, The by Nancy Farmer 7
Second Summer of the Sisterhood, The by Ann Brashares 11
Secret Hour, The by Scott Westerfeld 53
Secret Sacrament by Sherryl Jordan 4
Seer and the Sword, The by Victoria Hanley 4
Separate Peace, A by John Knowles 40
Seven Wise Princesses: A Medieval Persian Tale, The by Wafa Tarnowska 3
Sexy by Joyce Carol Oates 26
Shadow Baby by Alison McGhee 12
Shadow of a Doubt by S.L. Rottman 16
Shattered Mirror by Amelia Atwater-Rhodes 56
Shattering Glass by Gail Giles 39
Shooter by Walter Dean Myers 36
Shooting Monarchs by John Halliday 28
Silmarillion, The by J.R.R. Tolkien 4
Silver Kiss by Annette Curtis Klause 56
Simple Gift, The by Steven Herrick 24
Singing the Dogstar Blues by Alison Goodman 53
Singularity by William Sleator 66
Sleep Rough Tonight by Ian Bone 39
Smack by Melvin Burgess 33
Small Avalanches and Other Stories by Joyce Carol Oates 59
Small Eternities by Michael Lawrence 53
Small Rain by Madeleine L'Engle 31
Snow by Tracy Lynn 6
Soldier Boys by Dean Hughes 48
Soldier X by Don Wulffson 20
Someone Like You by Sarah Dessen 17
Something Wicked This Way Comes by Ray Bradbury 35
Sorceress by Celia Rees 8
Sorcery and Cecelia or the Enchanted Chocolate Pot: Being the Correspondence of Two Young Ladies of Quality Regarding Various Magical Scandals in London and the Country by Patricia C. Wrede 12
Speak by Laurie Halse Anderson 33
St. Michael's Scales by Neil Connelly 28
Stargirl by Jerry Spinelli 13
Stars of David: Prominent Jews Talk About Being Jewish by Abigail Pogrebin 63
Staying Fat for Sarah Byrnes by Chris Crutcher 42
Step from Heaven, A by An Na 48

Steroids and Your Muscles: The Incredible Disgusting Story by Albert Spring 25
Stoner and Spaz by Ron Koertge 15
Storyteller's Daughter, The by Cameron Dokey 3
Stotan by Chris Crutcher 26
*Straight Talk About Death for Teens: How to Cope with
    Losing Someone You Love* by Earl A. Grollman 72
Stravaganza: City of Masks by Mary Hoffman 27
Stuck in Neutral by Terry Trueman 68
Summerland by Michael Chabon 66
Sun Moon Stars Rain by Jan Cheripko 16
Sundiata: An Epic of Old Mali by D.T. Niane 54
Taker, The by Julia Steele 34
Tale of Paradise Lost: Based on the Poem by John Milton, The by Nancy Willard ...2
Target by Kathleen Jeffrie Johnson 61
Tears of the Salamander, The by Peter Dickinson 27
Teens and Cheating by Hal Marcovitz 34
Teens Cook: How to Cook What You Want to Eat by Megan Carle 65
Tenderness by Robert Cormier 61
Tenth Power, The by Kate Constable 23
Testimony of an Irish Slave Girl by Kate McCafferty 29
*There Is No Me without You: One Woman's Odyssey to
    Rescue Africa's Children* by Melissa Fay Greene 67
Things Change by Patrick Jones 49
Things Left Unsaid: A Novel in Poems by Stephanie Hemphill 24
Third Eye, The by Lois Duncan 10
This Side of Paradise by Steven L. Layne 1
This Strange New Feeling: Three Love Stories from Black History by Julius Lester ..54
Three Clams and an Oyster by Randy Powell 25
Tombs of Atuan, The by Ursula Le Guin 23
*Total Immersion: A Revolutionary Way to Swim
    Better and Faster* by Terry Laughlin 26
Trial of Witches, A by Ivan Bunn 44
Trickster's Choice by Tamora Pierce 23
Troublemakers by John McNally 57
Troy by Adele Geras 37
True and Faithful Narrative, A by Katherine Sturtevant 27
True Confessions of a Hollywood Starlet by Lola Douglas 73
True Meaning of Cleavage, The by Mariah Fredericks 34
*Truth About Sexual Behavior and
    Unplanned Pregnancy, The* by Elissa Howard-Barr 17
ttyl by Lauren Myracle 58
Unchosen: The Hidden Lives of Hasidic Rebels by Hella Winston 63
Under the Baseball Moon by John H. Ritter 73
Under the Wolf, Under the Dog by Adam Rapp 14
Underwood See, The by Michael Lawrence 53
Vampire Encyclopedia, The by Matthew Bunson 56

Vampireville by Ellen Schreiber 64
Voices of Rape by Janet Bode 18
Waifs and Strays by Charles de Lint 7
Waiting for Odysseus by Clemence McLaren 37
Wanderer, The by Sharon Creech 13
Wanted! by Caroline B. Cooney 10
War for the Oaks by Emma Bull 6
Waterless Sea, The by Kate Constable 23
What Happened to Lani Garner? by Carol Plum-Ucci 15
When Dad Killed Mom by Julius Lester 59
When Jeff Comes Home by Catherine Atkins 61
*When Parents Have Problems: A Book for Teens and Older Children
   with an Abusive, Alcoholic, or Mentally Ill Parent* by Susan B. Miller 60
Wicked Day, The by Mary Stewart 70
Whirligig by Paul Fleischman 52
White Oleander by Janet Fitch 59
Witch Ball by Linda Joy Singleton 62
Witch-Hunts: Mysteries of the Salem Witch Trials by Marc Aronson 44
Wrecked by E.R. Frank 33
Year the Gypsies Came, The by Linzi Glass 16
Yom Kippur a Go-Go: A Memoir by Matthue Roth 63
You Remind Me of You by Eireann Corrigan 24
Young Dancer's Apprenticeship, A by Olympia Dowd 21
Youth in Prison by Roger Smith 57

E. Subjects

Accidents 10, 22, 40, 43, 48, 53, 74
Acting 49, 63
Adoption 9, 26
African Americans 26, 29, 33, 54, 69
Africans 29, 54, 67
Alcohol Abuse 40, 48
Alcoholism 15, 19, 38, 60, 67
Animals 2, 50, 51
Art 21, 53
Attention Deficit Hyperactivity Disorder 5
Ballet 21
Basketball 68
Boarding Schools 12, 28, 40
Body Image 11, 21, 22, 31, 40, 42, 48, 49, 51, 52, 58, 59, 62, 65, 73
Brothers 16, 36, 68, 75
Brothers and Sisters 3, 9, 13, 14, 15, 16, 19, 24, 32, 39, 46, 66, 72, 73, 75
Bullying 20, 26, 32, 36, 41, 43, 49, 55, 58, 64
Cancer 11, 72

Censorship 27, 46
Child Abuse 26, 33, 48
Child Sexual Abuse 33, 61
Circuses 52
Cities 6, 7, 14, 22, 27, 30, 62, 63, 69
Cooking 65
Crime 16, 24, 36, 47, 57, 59, 61, 69
Crocodiles 50
Cults 5, 10, 62
Dancing 21, 22
Death 3, 16, 19, 28, 30, 35, 36, 38, 40, 43, 45, 46, 51, 53, 54, 57, 59, 61, 67, 69, 71, 72 74
Depression 24, 38, 43, 45, 71, 72, 74
Disabilities 23, 26, 32, 42, 52, 66, 68
Divorce 13, 32, 68
Dogs 45, 51
Drug Abuse 7, 14, 24, 25, 57, 61, 62, 69, 71
Ecology 51
Elderly 35, 45, 46, 60, 72
Elves 4, 6
Emotional Problems 9, 17, 24, 26, 33, 36, 38, 39, 40, 41, 42, 43, 44, 45, 47, 48, 55, 57, 58, 59, 60, 61, 66, 68
Fairies 6, 7, 44
Family Problems 5, 8, 11, 25, 27, 30, 38, 39, 46, 48, 49, 59, 62, 67, 71, 72, 73, 75
Fathers and Daughters 3, 8, 15, 27, 30, 44, 48, 54, 56, 62
Fathers and Sons 8, 20, 25, 26, 32, 34, 36, 49, 50, 51, 53, 57, 59, 68, 69, 70
Fires 19, 38, 41, 42, 43, 45, 46
Football 19, 25, 51
Foster Homes 26, 33, 41, 50
Friendship 7, 11, 12, 18, 19, 20, 22, 23, 25, 29, 30, 34, 40, 42, 43, 45, 46, 47, 49, 52, 55, 58, 62, 64, 65, 67, 68, 70, 72, 73, 74
Gangs 15, 55, 69
Genetics 1, 35, 51, 52
Ghosts 10, 12, 54, 71
Gods and Goddesses 37, 54
Grandparents 11, 46, 72
Grieving 9, 12, 19, 28, 35, 38, 43, 45, 46, 53, 54, 67, 72, 74
Gypsies 12, 16
High Schools 18, 19, 25, 26, 31, 32, 34, 36, 39, 41, 43, 47, 49, 55, 56, 58, 64, 69, 71
Hispanics 19, 32
HIV/AIDS 32, 67
Homosexuality 42, 55, 62
Illness 61, 66, 67, 72
Jealousy 22, 30, 37, 38, 46, 58, 62, 66, 70, 73, 74, 75

Jewish Americans 63
Jews 20, 46
Journals 1, 33, 59
Journeys 2, 3, 4, 7, 10, 11, 16, 17, 23, 29, 37, 46, 48, 51, 52, 53, 54, 59, 61, 67
Kidnapping 8, 10, 13, 57, 61
Knights and Knighthood 70
Learning Disabilities 5, 26, 32
Letter Writing 11, 38
Magic 3, 4, 6, 7, 10, 12, 23, 44, 52, 53, 54, 58, 62, 70
Medical Experimentation 35, 51
Medicine 4, 30, 44, 46, 67
Mental Illness 28, 33, 36, 38, 39, 43, 61
Mothers and Daughters 6, 7, 12, 17, 27, 31, 34, 35, 38, 46, 53, 56, 59, 60, 63, 67, 70, 72
Mothers and Sons 20, 28, 35, 53, 57
Moving 1, 6, 32, 36, 55, 56, 60, 63
Mummies 52
Murder 15, 16, 28, 30, 36, 46, 51, 56, 57, 59, 61, 69
Music 6, 14, 22, 23, 27, 31, 49, 62, 63
Native Americans 41, 56
Oceans 51
Occupations 4, 21, 22, 23, 27, 44, 63, 65
Opera 27, 31
Orphans 28, 41
Peer Pressure 15, 18, 19, 20, 21, 25, 26, 31, 32, 34, 36, 39, 40, 42, 49, 55, 56, 58, 64
Physically Handicapped 26, 68
Pregnancy 5, 17, 44, 54
Prejudices 1, 8, 10, 12, 15, 16, 19, 20, 21, 23, 26, 29, 32, 33, 41, 44, 46, 52, 54, 56, 67
Prison 57, 69
Prostitution 14, 61, 67
Race Relations 8, 19, 20, 26, 29, 32, 33, 54
Rape 2, 16, 29, 61
Relationships 4, 8, 14, 18, 19, 21, 23, 27, 30, 37, 39, 40, 41, 46, 48, 54, 55, 56, 63, 64, 69, 70, 71, 73, 74, 75
Religion 2, 5, 10, 20, 27, 44, 46, 48, 54, 63, 71, 72
Royalty 3, 4, 27, 30, 70
Runaways 5, 7, 14, 15, 17, 27, 29, 33, 52, 61, 62
Sailing 10, 23, 37
Self-Esteem 2, 5, 13, 17, 19, 21, 22, 23, 25, 26, 31, 34, 36, 37, 38, 39, 41, 42, 49, 55, 58, 59, 60, 62, 63, 65, 75
Sexual Assault 18, 27, 47
Sexual Relationships 5, 8, 9, 11, 17, 30, 39, 44, 48, 52, 60, 61, 62, 74, 75
Sexuality 9, 18, 73
Sisters 5, 17, 21, 22, 24, 38, 44, 45, 59

Skateboarding 73
Slavery 29, 54
Stepfamilies 11, 59
Stress 18, 19, 20, 21, 24, 25, 34, 50, 55, 57, 59, 60, 67, 68, 69, 72
Suicide 5, 9, 30, 33, 71
Summer Camps 11, 42
Survival 10, 45, 46, 51, 61, 67
Swimming 1, 26
Teachers 3, 12, 20, 21, 26, 28, 31, 51, 58, 71
Testing 1, 5, 18, 34
Theft 2, 17, 18, 21, 58, 62
Time Travel 10, 12, 51, 53, 62, 66
Trolls 7
Universities and Colleges 18, 19, 34
Vampires 56, 64
Violence 8, 10, 14, 15, 16, 20, 24, 26, 28, 30, 32, 33, 36, 39, 46, 50, 54, 55, 56, 57, 59, 61, 68, 69, 70, 75
War 1, 3, 4, 6, 20, 37, 70
Weight Control 22, 31, 65
Witchcraft 44, 58, 62, 70
Wizards 23, 70
Writing 1, 15, 33, 47, 59, 75

F. Genres

Adventure 3, 10, 23, 51
Fantasy 2, 3, 4, 6, 7, 10, 12, 23, 37, 44, 52, 53, 54, 56, 58, 62, 70
Historical 2, 12, 20, 27, 29, 30, 37, 44, 46, 52, 54, 70
Horror 35, 56, 58, 62, 64
Humor 11, 21, 63, 65
International 8, 10, 12, 14, 15, 16, 17, 20, 27, 28, 30, 37, 44, 46, 47, 50, 53, 55, 67, 70, 75
Multicultural 19, 26, 29, 32, 33, 54, 63, 69
Mystery 16, 21, 35, 38, 41, 50, 59
Poetry 24, 48, 75
Realistic 5, 9, 11, 13, 14, 15, 16, 17, 18, 19, 21, 22, 24, 25, 26, 28, 31, 32, 33, 34, 36, 38, 39, 40, 41, 42, 43, 47, 48, 49, 50, 55, 57, 59, 60, 61, 63, 65, 67, 68, 69, 72, 73, 74, 75
Religious 2, 5, 27, 44, 46, 48, 72
Romance 4, 27, 30, 37, 46, 56, 65
Science Fiction 1, 8, 45, 51, 53, 66
Sports 11, 25, 26, 68
Supernatural 3, 10, 12, 44, 52, 54, 56, 58, 62, 71
Suspense 15, 16, 24, 27, 38, 39, 43, 50, 51, 56, 59

G. Curriculum Connections

Art 4, 6, 12, 43, 61
Biology 3, 5, 18, 25, 35, 38, 42, 50, 51, 59, 66
Career Education 22, 34, 60, 65
Creative Writing 9, 17, 19, 24, 28, 30, 37, 40, 48
Drama 17, 30, 37
English 2, 4, 8, 9, 11, 12, 17, 19, 24, 28, 30, 33, 37, 40, 47, 48, 49, 56, 61, 62, 69, 70, 71, 74
Foreign Languages 11, 54
Geography 1, 10, 23, 41, 50, 51, 54, 64, 66
Health 3, 5, 14, 18, 21, 25, 26, 32, 38, 39, 42, 59, 67, 68
History 1, 2, 6, 8, 10, 16, 20, 23, 27, 29, 31, 33, 37, 41, 43, 44, 45, 46, 47, 52, 54, 55, 56, 57, 62, 63, 64, 69, 70, 71
Life Skills 60, 65
Math 60
Music 27, 31, 72
Physical Education 13, 21, 26, 73
Physics 53
Psychology 7, 8, 9, 14, 22, 26, 28, 35, 36, 39, 44, 49, 55, 56, 57, 58, 59, 68, 72, 74, 75
Science 3, 5, 10, 14, 15, 25, 26, 35, 38, 42, 45, 50, 51, 53, 66
Sociology 7, 16, 22, 33, 41, 49, 55, 56, 57, 58, 63, 64, 67

Appendix
Student Evaluation Form

On the next page is the form students use in my graduate level Young Adult Literature course. They add their five booktalked titles.

Booktalk Evaluation Form

Date: _____ Grade: _____ Subject: _____ M or F (circle one)

Booktalk Topic: _____

                                                                (circle one)

1. Did you enjoy listening to the booktalks?   Y   N

2. Have you ever listened to a booktalk before?   Y   N

3. Would you like to hear more booktalks?   Y   N

4. Which one of the following was your *favorite* type of booktalk?
   - A. First person (when I talked like one of the characters in the book)
   - B. Excerpt (when I read aloud a portion of the book)
   - C. Discussion (when I just talked about the book)

5. Which one of the following was your *least favorite* type of booktalk?
   - A. First person (when I talked like one of the characters in the book)
   - B. Excerpt (when I read aloud a portion of the book)
   - C. Discussion (when I just talked about the book)

6. Of the five books that were booktalked, which one are you *most* likely to read?
   - A.
   - B.
   - C.
   - D.
   - E.

7. Of the five books that were booktalked, which one are you *least* likely to read?
   - A.
   - B.
   - C.
   - D.
   - E.

8. What types of materials do you usually read for pleasure? (circle as many as apply)

Mysteries	Sports Novels	Informational Books
Historical Fiction	Adventure/Survival Novels	Newspapers
Fantasy	Romance Novels	Magazines
Horror/Supernatural	Short Stories	Graphic Novels (comics)
Science Fiction	Religious/Spiritual Novels	Computer/Electronic Game Materials
Realistic Modern Fiction	Biographies	Other (write below)

Please add your comments to the back of this sheet. Thank you!

www.ingramcontent.com/pod-product-compliance
Lightning Source LLC
Chambersburg PA
CBHW080541300426
44111CB00017B/2823